Paul's Response to the Roman World:
The Gospel Confronted Paganism

(Volume One)

By Dr. Randall D. Smith

Paul's Response to the Roman World:
The Gospel Confronted Paganism

Preface

These volumes were prepared with students and teachers of the Bible in mind. The series is taken from the actual teaching notes of Dr. Smith as he teaches through all of the Bible each year at Great Commission Bible Institute in Sebring, Florida.

Examining the Life of the Apostle Paul from his birth in Tarsus of Cilicia to his beheading outside of the city of Rome is essential for any maturing follower of Jesus Christ. This volume will help you begin that journey. It includes the background materials on who the Apostle was and what God accomplished in and through his life from his birth until he completed the second mission journey – arguably the worst time in his life. These studies remind us that Paul was an excellent combination of a Roman structured mind, an accomplished Greek reader and speaker, and a throbbing Hebrew heart. God used a unique man to accomplish a mammoth task – explain the Gospel of grace when God replaced the former atonement system with a full justification by a completed work in Messiah.

Table of Contents

Paul's Response to the Roman World

Part One: Background for the study of Paul in the context of the Roman world.

- What do we mean by "Roman"?
- What are the sources of information for that period?
- What were Roman values?
- Where does Paul fit in the Roman timeline?
- What did Paul write?
- Who was Nero and what happened between the Emperor and Paul?
- Who were Paul's friends and acquaintances?
- What is the Book of Acts and how does it fit into the New Testament?

Paul's Response to the Roman World:
"Paul in the context of the Roman world"

When we speak of the "Romans" we are, in fact, speaking of many people groups without a *common ancestry*, a singular *common religious belief* system, or even a *singular alphabet*. We are speaking of a vast empire that began as one city and one tribe, but eventually swallowed up many people and even much older empires. As they amalgamated them into the Roman world they worked to give the people a common sense of identity, a "Roman world view." Every great empire that preceded Rome since the Old Kingdom of Egypt dynasties of 2600 BCE and the Akkadian Empire of Mesopotamia in 2300 BCE had *at least* a common script with which to communicate to their various subjects or citizens. Rome had conquered so vast a territory on three continents that no singular alphabet existed. Besides that, scholars estimate the population's literacy rate at only about ten percent (10%)!

One could say that the chief accomplishment, then, of the Roman system of governance that was engineered by Caesar Augustus and carried by a series of Senate bodies and Imperial personages, was that of forming a sense of **cohesion and identity** across an Empire. Look at the size of the cohesiveness problem:

- There was no common national heritage defined by land; nor was there a common history to cite and rally people.

- There was no natural singular language or script on which to base one's identity.

- The land mass of even the Italic Peninsula was separated by major mountain chains such as the Pyrenees, the Alps, etc. As the empire grew, much of it was formed around the Mediterranean Sea.

The Roman's came up with an elegant solution that changed people's hearts without becoming an overt political move: they began stamping cultural cues on the people – literally "pressing them into a mold." The master brilliance behind their work was the fact that the objective was hidden in plain sight.

In order to build a sense of common identity necessary to hold the society together, Roman leaders devised a very intention set of reproducible monuments and events and spread them across the vast empire. In fact one scholar noted: "Paul's world was largely defined by deliberate cultural cues," argues Dr. Steven Tuck of Miami University, "placed strategically and at great cost to the Roman citizenry by their masters." These had an essential purpose, which was to bring solidarity to the world while celebrating the "Roman way" of doing things. This method was, in essence, change by popularization, and it was done in at least ten important ways:

- First, **defining urban spaces** in such a way that a Roman would feel a city was familiar from one end of the empire to the other.

- Second, **standardizing dress** among the class structures – so that a Roman of an elevated class would be easily identifiable in their toga on sight, or possibly by a medallion on closer inspection.

- Third, **creating an array of** "**liminal monuments**" at ports throughout the Roman world – a series of statues, markers and monuments that helped a Roman always feel he was traveling "in Rome" while on *Mare Nostrum* ("Our Sea" or the Mediterranean Sea as the Romans referred to it).

- Fourth, the **creation and development of public spectacles** including "*pompa processions*" of victory and the like to allow a Roman to relive the glorious past of Rome in any province.

- Fifth, "ludi" or **games and contests** that were designed to allow the regional and city rivalries to take on a consistent Roman flavor.

- Sixth, the **defining of domus (home) markers and interior spaces** – from an etched wreath or "civic crown" above a door or a bench beside the front door to the defined public porches inside the home that were open to visitors and allowed people to recognize the status of a patron visually.

- Seventh, a **recognizable legal system** that allowed a Roman to feel "under the law" of Rome at any place in the Empire.

- Eighth, a **Temple system that spread coinage** as tokens with carefully crafted messages about the Roman *Princeps* or Roman values, so the citizen felt that the Emperor was bringing stability to the region where he lived.

- Ninth, the **Roman army** and its symbols helped a citizen feel protected and unified.

- Tenth, a **Roman census, forum weights** (of the city "Aediles" or city managers) **and a taxation** system that allowed the citizenry to interact with Rome on the level of local projects that were paid via the tax system.

The fact is the most important Roman objective was to homogenize the population and allow people to become either "citizens of Rome" or "hopeful to become citizens of Rome." The swift and full assimilation of the Romans became a platform for the swift move from paganism to Christianity in western history. In many ways one mimicked the other. That is one reason it is so important to study Roman history and set Paul within that context.

A second reason for the study of the Roman world of Paul moves us in a different direction, but can also be found in the historical data of the period: Rome reminds us that politicians and social change activists can also learn the lesson – **you can entertain people into a new set of beliefs and even a new set of ethical presuppositions.**

A third reason to study the Roman period surrounding Paul's travels and writing is to gain a clearer understanding of the text of the New Testament. The key to being able to **unlock the**

imagery that was common to Paul and his contemporaries – is found in **exposing the lives of people that read the initial letters** – the slaves that huddled in the secret places to hear the message of Jesus as told by the Apostle to the Gentiles. Slaves weren't alone in those meetings – there were also men and women of substance – those from the upper classes (*honestiores*), as well as criminals (like Onesimus), and occasional legionary or auxiliary soldier, some prostitutes and perhaps even the lowest of all orders – actors and celebrities (*infamii*)!

The quest of a study of the life and ministry of Paul must include an understanding of the "Roman world view" in order to help a student grapple with the challenge of carrying the Gospel into that time and place. What were the implications of "coming to Jesus" for each of the people in the gathering I just mentioned above?

Rome was a constructed blend of people that was held together by intentional social engineering – and became a society sensitive about place and propriety. In such a **status conscious society**, how could a Roman woman of "substance" **accept the instruction to place little emphasis on her hair plating?** How would an **equestrian deal with sitting beside a slave in an 'agape meal'** at the behest of an early church leader? Could a **slave who worked in a brothel** *really* be accepted as a **full sister** in Messiah? Could a **brutal gladiator or silly mime actor really be accepted into the body of Christ?**

These were first century problems, and Paul's handling of them set the pattern for moving the Gospel into the pagan world of first century Romans. Exploring the lives of various kinds of Romans can help us grapple with the successful methods of expansion of the message of Jesus in the first century – but it will do *more*. It will also challenge us in our love, acceptance and outreach with the Gospel in an increasingly pagan "post-Christian" western world.

Paul's Response to the Roman World: Sources for Exposing the Roman World

The Bible did not take place in a vacuum; the history of events in the period surrounding the writings has other collaborating sources that can be valuable to the modern Bible student. It is not essential to fully grasp the whole of the period (if that is even possible) to have God **use** the text of Scripture in your life, but it is helpful to be at least briefly familiarized with some of the source materials we use to understand the meaning of common jargon and objects found in the New Testament.

"Pauline history" is properly a subset of what scholars would normally call **Roman Imperial history**. The Republican era of Rome dates from about 509-31 BCE, and the most violent political upheavals in Roman history occurred at the end of that period. Following the overthrow of Senate oligarchical rule, a series of "***Princeps***" or Roman emperors took over (31 BCE-476 CE). Our specific study is most concerned with sources dated between Caesar Augustus (31 BCE-14 CE) to Constantine (C4th CE) – during the church's formative period. In order to study that period, we will gaze at a series of biographic portraits, sometimes encompassing vast achievement and at other times shocking us with some of the darkest depravities.

A Quick View of the History:

To recap, Roman imperial history does not refer to the period of Rome's **territorial** supremacy, which was established under the republic, but to governance by the emperors that supplanted the republican oligarchy. The complex history of this period alternated between stable dynasties and periods of civil war, eventually ending in sustained chaos:

- Garrett Fagan, a scholar on the Roman world, has said in numerous classes: "Between Augustus (31 BCE) and Severus Alexander (who was murdered by his own troops in 235 CE), there were **24** legitimate emperors, with the length of their reigns ranging from Augustus's 45 years to the 66-day rule of Didius Julianus.

- The 50 years that followed Severus Alexander saw even greater instability: It saw some **21** legitimate emperors (all but three perished violently) and **38** usurpers (who all perished at the hands of legitimate authority).

- Diocletian re-established order (285-305 CE) and things settled down for a time."

Dr. Garrett G. Fagan, Professor of Ancient History at Penn State (read anything he writes on the Roman world!) notes the time was turbulent, and suggests that it was perhaps as dangerous to be found in the home of the Emperor as to be a Roman legionary. Ancient life wasn't for the weak-willed and slow minded- they were often abused and plowed under.

How do we know about this time period? It is a fair question that should be explored. We need to place the New Testament in the context of contemporaries, and in many cases, our arguments are measurably stronger if those sources cannot be linked to the cause of the Gospel. Secularists will find such evidence much more compelling.

Scholars primarily turn to the use of four primary sources of Roman History:

- Literary sources: contemporary writings by historical figures.
- Epigraphy: Inscriptions on monuments and the like.
- Numismatic evidence: coins and their well-crafted messages.
- Physical finds: archaeological sites.

Each of these contain a varied set of strengths and limitations inherent in their form. It is important for a student of the Bible to really appreciate these source materials available for the study of the Roman emperors, but also recognize the burden of strict limitations they carry.

- For the periods of Augustus and the whole Julio-Claudian Dynasty that followed him (31 BCE to 68 CE), scholars possess relatively full written accounts, supplemented by coins and inscriptions. This richness, at least at this stage, "thins out" with the Flavian Dynasty (69–96 CE) and runs out entirely for Trajan and much of the C2nd CE. For that era, modern students are forced to rely entirely on Byzantine summaries of lost earlier works as well as contemporary coins and inscriptions.

- With the rise of Marcus Aurelius, Commodus, and the Severan Dynasty that followed (c.160–235 CE), literary evidence again becomes much more plentiful, and is properly supplemented by coins and inscriptions. A dark curtain appears to descend again for much of the C3rd CE, until Diocletian and Constantine (early C4th CE).

Again I borrow from Dr. Garrett G. Fagan as I paraphrase from his courses on ancient Rome: "The most directly pertinent **literary sources** for the emperors are often those polished, essentially *artificial* works of literature composed by ancient Romans and preserved by a process of copying through the centuries. Their weaknesses stem from the fact that they are strictly from the upper classes and most were composed by men, most who lived in Rome. It is, thus, bounded by class, gender, and geography. Our best literary sources for emperors would be imperial memoirs but only two emperors have left us works by their own hands: Augustus and Marcus Aurelius – the rest were lost in history." Here is a brief list the Penn State scholar offers:

- Of these, the greatest is Cornelius **Tacitus** (c. 56–120), who wrote the Histories and the Annals

- As a secretary to Hadrian, Gaius **Suetonius** Tranquillus (c. 70–130) wrote biographical portraits known today as The Twelve Caesars, stretching from Julius Caesar to Domitian.

- Lucius Cassius **Dio** (c. 164–230) composed a global history of Rome in 80 books.

- For many of the 3rd-century emperors down to Diocletian, we encounter what is perhaps the strangest source in all of ancient history: the **Historia Augusta**

- Lucius Annaeus **Seneca** (c. 4 BCE-65 CE) was deeply embedded in the Julio-Claudian Dynasty. His literary output was impressive, including letters, tragedies, speeches, and philosophical treatises.

- The major literary contribution of **Pliny the Younger** (c. 61–112) is a collection of stylized letters published in 10 books, which are excellent documents for the Roman senatorial lifestyle and sensibilities of his day.

In addition to literary sources, it is important to recall that ancient Mediterranean cultures inscribed important engravings on stone. **Inscriptions** relevant to the study of emperors include epitaphs of dead emperors and members of the imperial house, senatorial decrees, imperial rescripts or edicts, decrees of local authorities, and sometimes, copies of correspondence between local communities and emperors. Particularly noteworthy are lists of **consuls,** termed *fasti*, with notations of historical events appended as they occurred. These were erected in Rome and other cities. Another useful source is the so-called **Acts of the Arval Brethren**, whose minutes, carved on stone, survive in fragments and record such events as imperial births and deaths, conspiracies uncovered, and so on.

Roman imperial **coins** were minted under state contracts and paid primarily to soldiers. On the obverse side of the coin is usually found the head of the emperor in profile. On the reverse is found the "message" of the coin: symbolic images, usually accompanied by text. A series of coins can confirm and corroborate the accounts in the literary sources, but such neat convergences are the exception.

Finally, we turn to **archaeological evidence**, that is, the remains of buildings erected by and for the Emperors. These are mostly found at Rome itself, the chief beneficiary of the resident emperor's largesse.

Paul's Response to the Roman World:
Thinking like a Roman

A Roman wasn't a person who lived in Rome, and perhaps had never been to Rome. Most "Romans" never stood in the Forum Romana, and never heard the roar of the crowd of the Circus Maximus. The concept of "Being a Roman" was more a cultural identity than a mere citizenship in an empire! The cultural identity can be seen in closer observation of "Roman period sites" that modern travelers can visit. Let's look more closely at some of the ideas behind the cultural identity, and offer some brief application of them to the New Testament issues of Paul's day:

Characteristic One - Common Identity:

Roman domination stretched from Scotland to Saudi Arabia at its height, but the majority of its inhabitants were illiterate. They were united in one government, but had no singular common alphabet, no singular language, and a vast array of religious and social traditions. Geography prevented its own division challenges - mountain ranges such as the Pyrenes, the Alps, the Pindos Mountains, and the Taurus Mountains kept the people apart. This made **symbolic and visual communication critical**.

One planned way to pass values was through a series of intentional **spectacles** - public events planned to knit the people together into a single empire. Another way to do that was a **common name system**. Engineering **common harbors and city plans** also helped. Reinforcing the **order of social status** was also essential. In fact, in most any public building, the space and context of the event helped to define the importance and standing of each of the parties involved in the event.

For instance, in Rome's "Flavian Amphitheatre" (Colloseo), we are confronted with the reality of class distinction. There was a **specific pattern to the seating**, suggesting the importance of those in that section. Additionally, there were those infamous (or "*novi infamii*"), who were in the **center of the arena as**

notorious people. An Emperor would not be found in the center of the arena, for his status would be affronted by such a display.

The writer Vitruvius, who lived in 27 BCE, explained the use of both domestic and public space in his architectural work. From works like his, we now understand more about the up society's normative behavior. In addition, from excavations such as those at Pompeii, we can now walk within the restored visual cues of that ancient architecture. For example:

- **Benches outside of a house** provide evidence the home was that of a patron.

- The **insignia of a civic crown** above the door of a home suggests the building howls one who was awarded by the state for civil or military accomplishment.

- By close examination of the ancient homes, we find that domestic space was not private in the modern sense.

We are privileged to have "keys" provided through archaeology as well as literary sources, coinage, and specific pieces of artwork that reveal daily life that have long been forgotten.

- Coinage of the ancient world reveals a number of important **priorities**. Some virtues such as **manliness** and **piety** are often celebrated on coinage because the money was given to widows and orphans.

- Today we would use a **press conference** to advertise what the Romans simply stamp on a **coin** and distribute.

In one sense, the common identity of Romans probably helped Paul explain the common identity believers found in Messiah:

1 Corinthians 12:13 "For by one Spirit we were all baptized into one body, whether Jews or Greeks, whether slaves or free, and we were all made to drink of one Spirit."

Ephesians 4:4 [There is] one body and one Spirit, just as also you were called in one hope of your calling; 5 one Lord, one faith, one baptism, 6 one God and Father of all who is over all and through all and in all.

The Roman Name is another example of "standardization." When one is operating a massive administrative load and jurisprudence system - individual identity quickly becomes important.

The names were formulaic, indicating individual identity and rank of social stratification. Every **male Roman** had at least one primary name called the **praenomen**. Normally it was only used within a family and in very familiar relationships. Romans had a VERY SMALL LIST they tended to choose from (and new names were suspect). Certainly the attitude of Zacharias and Elizabeth's neighbors seem to reflect this – though they were also Jews – Lk. 1:63).

Beyond the **PRAENOMEN** (personal name), Roman citizens had a **NOMEN** which identified their GENS or CLAN. Adoption into a family was literally adoption into a gens – and was a key identifier of both character and relationship (Ephesians 1:11). Works of each generation were COMBINED to show the continuing character of the gens – and may be at the heart of a claim like in Matthew 7:22 "did we not work in your name?"

Elite clans used a **COGNOMEN** to denote the branch of the gens from which they came – in particular use by aristocratic families.

Celebrity Romans had a fourth name – the **COGNOMEN EX VIRTUTE** – not normally passed beyond one generation and used as a marking of individual celebrity or rank. This is a form of ABSOLUTE PRAISE, and helps us understand the notion of Philippians 2:9 "God highly exalted Him and gave Him a name above all names."

A praenomen / nomen / cognomen: **Gaius Julius Caesar**
A praenomen / nomen / cognomen / cog ex virtute:
Publius Cornelius Sulla Felix
Publius Cornelius Scipio Africanus

Women in a Roman were often all named by the same praenomen. Until quite late in Roman history, there were **no real girls' names**. One from the Julian clan (or **gens Julia**) would be simply called "Julia" whereas one from the Claudian clan (**gens Claudia**) would be called simply "Claudia",etc. An older sister would be called "Julia major" or "Claudia major" and a younger sister would be "Julia minor" or "Claudia minor". An even older or younger sister would be called "Julia maxima" or "Julia minima". By this, we assume that a woman's social identity was greatly defined by her relationships - being first a daughter and then a wife.

The Roman Date reflects in a small way the value system of the people under our study. In American life we use the **Christian religion** as the source for our dating. The ancient Romans used two things for dating –

- **Governing personalities** for their dating purposes, as in the **year of a consulship**.

- The **date from the founding of Rome**. This demonstrated the primacy of government and collective identity over other cultural concerns.

Characteristic Two – Expansive Citizenry

The term "Roman" is problematic because it changed its meaning over time. The original designation "Roman" meant "being a native of the city of Rome." By around 300 BCE however, when Rome completed the conquest of the adjacent territories of Latium, Roman citizenship extended to the other Latins (a linguistic designation). When the "Latin Romans" expanded beyond their region, they increasingly extended "citizenship" to the people they conquered. By 212 CE, Emperor Caracalla granted citizenship to **every free man living within the borders of the Roman Empire**.

This was a unique strategy for the ancients, and it constantly redefined what it meant to be Roman. In fact, the idea of people from a variety of geographical backgrounds and language groups becoming on new nation was perhaps not really tried again until the British colonial period, or the experiment of America begun nearly 2,000 years later. Some may argue the Egyptians, and perhaps Mesopotamians had, on occasion, viewed themselves as one people – but the kingdoms were much smaller and the populations not nearly as diverse.

Let's not overplay this. Citizenship did not destroy informal racial prejudice but all Romans, whatever their ethnicity, had the **benefits of territorial security** and **celebrated the same services** characteristic of Roman civility. As a Roman, you believed in the rightness of slavery, as did most ancient societies. You offered one unique twist: You saw it in your interest to grant citizenship to slaves. Manumission had never existed on the scale that Rome offered and never offered the same opportunities for advancement and enrichment. Not all slaves were eligible to acquire rights but a sizeable proportion, notably domestic slaves were given that opportunity.

Paul knew that his citizenship afforded him certain treatments, and he made use of his identity when the time was right. When he was seized at the Temple in Jerusalem, he used knowledge of the rights of citizens to be released from bonds.

*Acts 22:28 The commander answered, "I acquired this citizenship with a large sum of money." And Paul said, "But **I was actually born [a citizen].**" 29 Therefore those who were about to examine him **immediately let go of him**; and the commander also was **afraid when he found out that he was a Roman**, and because he had put him in chains.*

At the same time, Paul encouraged believers to see the primary prize of citizenship as above, and not on the earth, as in:

*Philippians 3:17 Brethren, join in following my example, and observe those who walk according to the pattern you have in us. 18 For many walk, of whom I often told you, and now tell you even weeping, [that they are] enemies of the cross of Christ, 19 whose end is destruction, whose god is [their] appetite, and [whose] glory is in their shame, who set their minds on earthly things. 20 **For our citizenship is in heaven, from*** *which also we eagerly wait for a Savior, the Lord Jesus Christ; 21 who will transform the body of our humble state into conformity with the body of His glory, by the exertion of the power that He has even to subject all things to Himself.*

Characteristic Three - Belief in "Roman Exceptionalism":

Romans felt they were subduing disorder and bringing civilization to the world – and they were destined to do so. Roman's largely believed they were performing vital peacekeeping roles in the world. To civilize the disorder, it became necessary to impose the same language, legal system, and sense of a "standard of living" on millions of people in areas like sanitation and community planning.

In Virgil's Aeneid, (written in the time of Augustus) the hero Aeneas went down to Hades to see his father, Anchises. His father offered him a prophetic preview of sorts to the founding of Rome and its destiny. Anchises gave definition to Rome's mission: (Latin: *"parcere subjectis et debellare superbos).* That is: "to humble the proud and spare the subjected." It *seems* entirely appropriate to refer to the Aeneid for a primer on Roman mentality because most read the poem at school or with tutor from the time of Augustus onward. It had as much impact on virtue and thought as Vitruvius had on building style from the same period.

Clearly the Romans thought they brought order from chaos, civility from barbarism, peace from anarchy and subdued nature to more easily accommodate the needs of people on earth. They saw themselves as the highest form – projecting power and order that resolved the problems of the world by might. Paul used this imagery when describing the work of Messiah over the world system – and it was sensible imagery to them. The tender images of Jesus were moved to more militant and power oriented images of **TRIUMPHALISM** as the Gospel spread among the Romans:

Ephesians 1:18 [I pray that] the eyes of your heart may be enlightened, so that you will know what is the hope of His calling, what are the riches of the glory of His inheritance in the saints, 19 and what is the surpassing greatness of His power toward us who believe. [These are] in accordance with the working of the strength of His might 20 which He brought about in Christ, when He raised Him from the dead and seated Him at His right hand in the heavenly [places], 21 far above all rule and authority and power and dominion, and every name that is named, not only in this age but also in the one to come. 22 And He put all things in subjection under His feet, and gave Him as head over all things to the church..."

Colossians 1:13 For He rescued us from the domain of darkness, and transferred us to the kingdom of His beloved Son, 14 in whom we have redemption, the forgiveness of sins. 15 He is the image of the invisible God, the firstborn of all creation. 16 For by Him all things were created, [both] in the heavens and on earth, visible and invisible, whether thrones or dominions or rulers or authorities-- all things have been created through Him and for Him. 17 He is before all things, and in Him all things hold together.

Colossians 3:1 Therefore if you have been raised up with Christ, keep seeking the things above, where Christ is, seated at the right hand of God. 2 Set your mind on the things above, not on the things that are on earth. 3 For you have died and your life is hidden with Christ in God. 4 When Christ, who is our life, is revealed, then you also will be revealed with Him in glory.

Characteristic Four - Adherence to Roman Virtues:

Beneath all the individual differences and class distinctions, there were common moral and ethical values that each generation of Romans was challenged to attempt to demonstrate in accepted behaviors. What were those virtues?

Fides: "**faithfulness**," seeing a difficult task through to completion – and not quitting. Paul prized the value of faithfulness, as he shared many times:

Ephesians 1:1 Paul, an apostle of Christ Jesus by the will of God, To the saints who are at Ephesus and [who are] **faithful** *in Christ Jesus. Colossians 1:2 To the saints and* **faithful** *brethren in Christ [who are] at Colossae: Grace to you and peace from God our Father.*

Wirtus: (virtue): is "**manliness**" seen through extraordinary acts of bravery or extreme prowess in battle. Displays of it led to promotions and rewards in society – political appointments, etc. Soldiers sought opportunities to fight in individual combat to display this. In Acts 23:11 Paul was before the Sanhedrin council at Jerusalem and said:

*"But on the night [immediately] following, the Lord stood at his side and said, "**Take courage**; for as you have solemnly witnessed to My cause at Jerusalem, so you must witness at Rome also."*

In Acts 27:22, 25 Paul demonstrated Roman virtues in the face of adversity: 22" [Yet] now I urge you to keep up your courage, for there will be no loss of life among you, but [only] of the ship.... 25 "Therefore, keep up your courage, men, for I believe God that it will turn out exactly as I have been told.

Part of the work of the legionnaire was to spread the notion of WIRTUS to the world – a chief visual cue to Romanization. Roman citizens learned and celebrated the achievements of the army, looking at insignias as some sports uniforms would be identified today!

One great example of "wirtus" can be noted in a well-known five hundred year old anecdote passed from Livy in about 27 BCE (in "Ab urbe condita libri" — from the founding of the city — a monumental history of ancient Rome in Latin. He told the tale of the young **Gaius Mucius Scaevola** and his bravery. In 508 BCE, during a war between Rome and Clusium, the Clusian king Lars Porsena laid siege to Rome. Young Gaius gained approval of the Roman Senate to slip into the Etruscan camp and attempt to murder Porsena. Because it was the soldiers' pay day, the king was dressed very similarly to his scribe – and killed Porsena's scribe instead of the king. On public trial, he placed his hand in a fire and held it there while it burned, uttering the immortal words, "Civis Romanus sum ... et facere et pati fortia Romanum est —"**I am a Roman citizen ... it is the characteristic of a Roman both to act and to suffer bravely**." He reportedly added that another three hundred Romans stood outside the camp with the same wirtus and determination - and he was released as a gesture of respect. Paul did seem somewhat concerned that he **not shame his Lord** in his **courage** in places like:

Philippians 1: 20 ...according to my earnest expectation and hope, that I will not be put to shame in anything, but [that] with all boldness, Christ will even now, as always, be exalted in my body, whether by life or by death.

Pietas: "piety," but should be more thought of as simply "**doing the right thing**" whether for parents, country, dead ancestors or your family's gods. It was a form of purity of ideals. "*Sum pius Aeneas*" is how Aeneas proudly introduces himself at the beginning of the poem. One famous image of pietas is when Aeneus was fleeing from the rubble of Troy, he was carrying his father Anchises on his back and clasping the hand of his little son Ascanius, while Anchises is clutching an image of the *penates* - the household gods rescued from Troy. The Aeneid was identified by Romans as an intensely moral poem, but it questions the value of the sacrifice that Aeneas and others must make to achieve an empire. Thinking of proper behavior, Peter wrote in:

1 Peter 1:15 but like the Holy One who called you, be holy yourselves also in all [your] behavior; 16 because it is written, "YOU SHALL BE HOLY, FOR I AM HOLY."

Family honor: The specific nature of the "*familia*" was a bit different than ours – as it included not only your immediate family, but also your extended family and dependents, both slave and free. Free dependents were "*clients*" who looked to the father of the family as their "*patronus*" or patron for support and protection. Also included were divine members – the *penates*, or family deities. One famous anecdote of family honor involved the wife of a Roman nobleman called Lucretia, told from the end of the monarchy period (509 BCE). Lucretia was raped by the king's son. A day later she appeared before her husband dressed in black, made him swear to take vengeance and told him of the crime – but promptly stabbed herself to death with a dagger. This tale would have been widely known from childhood onward, and it aptly illustrates that an honorable death would have been revered over a life of shame – though moderns can understand clearly the rapist is the one that should have felt all the shame. The story of Masada as told by Josephus would have drawn a nod of respect from the victorious Romans – and was included to boost the honor of the victory over the Jews. Paul argued from common honor in places like

1 Corinthians 11:1 Be imitators of me, just as I also am of Christ....14 Does not even nature itself teach you that if a man has long hair, it is a dishonor to him...

Traditions: No simple term like "conservative" could come close to Roman respect for tradition. There was no constitution in Rome – but there was a propriety of the way things "should be done" and that was largely set by the ancestors as seen in the Latin phrase "*mos maiorum*" or "the customs of the greater ones." Romans revered their ancestors, sought to emulate them, and looked to them for guidance and support. They forged a link of chain that you joined and added to with children. The Romans DID have some flexibility in practical matters, but sought to keep the INTENT of the fathers in all things. Remember, the original Romans were reasonably isolated and "upstream thinkers" – that adapted to the "downstream" thinking later on.

Gravitas: or "seriousness," was a distinctly Roman virtue that kept them from smiling in portraits for generations! The opposite or "*levitas*" was the mark of an inferior mind (sadly used to describe women in the period). Paul reflected this to Titus in:

Titus 2:2 Older men are to be temperate, dignified, sensible, sound in faith, in love, in perseverance...7 in

all things show yourself to be an example of good deeds, [with] purity in doctrine, dignified...

Characteristic Five - State Tribal Thinkers:

The Roman value of the *"res publica"* or "common wealth" affected dramatically their willingness to serve and preserve the state. Romans believed themselves bound by duty to the common wealth or "republic," in ways that would seem extreme to us today. When Lucius Iunius Brutus liberated Rome from the rule of the kings allegedly in 509 BCE, he became one of the first two consuls in the republic. The people swore an oath to resist anyone who would subjugate them and reign as king again. After some time, monarchists formed a conspiracy and Brutus had them all executed, **including his own sons and brothers**. He saw the *res publica* as greater than the *familia*.

The community was not only valued, it was close quartered and very PUBLIC. The premium moderns place on PRIVACY was not known in the ancient world. There is no real privacy in a **slave society**, for they know your most intimate secrets. Add to that, Rome lacked modern plumbing and the need to relieve one's self outside the home was a public act. Even latrines didn't have stalls, and a visit was a social event, froth with conversations with the person sitting beside you. It doesn't appear that men and women were always in separate facilities. In Herculaneum a latrine was found adjacent to the men's bath house, but none with the women's bathhouse - which have led some to suggest that women were forced at times to share the same facilities as men, or had specific times for using the limited facilities. This may account for women always leaving the table in the restaurant together in modern times, but who can really tell?

The writer of Hebrews stated that behavior must be measured against the community, and that our actions are to be based on the community of faith to which we belong.

Hebrews 12:1 Therefore, since we have so great a cloud of witnesses surrounding us, let us also lay aside every encumbrance and the sin which so easily entangles us, and let us run with endurance the race that is set before us...22 But you have come to Mount Zion and to the city of the living God, the heavenly Jerusalem, and to myriads of angels, 23 to the general assembly and church of the firstborn who are enrolled in heaven, and to God, the Judge of all, and to the spirits of [the] righteous made perfect...

Paul frequently addressed the believers as part of the community church of their locale, such as in 1 Corinthians 1:1-3:

"Paul, called [as] an apostle of Jesus Christ by the will of God, and Sosthenes our brother, 2 To the church of God which is at Corinth, to those who have been sanctified in Christ Jesus, saints by calling, with all who in every place call on the name of our Lord Jesus Christ, their [Lord] and ours: 3 Grace to you and peace from God our Father and the Lord Jesus Christ."

Characteristic Six - Amended Caste System:

In every public space, being "in one's place" was reinforced. Dress, seating arrangements and even entrances and exits were markers of social status. Roman life was a very status conscious life.

Galatians 3:26 For you are all sons of God through faith in Christ Jesus. 27 For all of you who were baptized into Christ have clothed yourselves with Christ. 28 There is neither Jew nor Greek, there is neither slave nor free man, there is neither male nor female; for you are all one in Christ Jesus.

*Ephesians 2:14 For He Himself is our peace, who made both [groups into] one and broke down the barrier of the dividing wall, 15 by abolishing in His flesh the enmity, [which is] the Law of commandments [contained] in ordinances, so that in Himself He might **make the two into one new man**, [thus] establishing peace,*

Characteristic Seven - Culturally Adaptive:

Romans blended the art, architecture and public education of those they conquered in a unique way. Even in something as central as religion – Rome borrowed her gods. More Romans followed gods of foreign origin than of their forefathers by the time of the spreading of the Gospel.

Colossians 3:9 Do not lie to one another, since you laid aside the old self with its [evil] practices, 10 and have put on the new self who is being renewed to a true knowledge according to the image of the One who created him-- 11 [a renewal] in which there is no [distinction between] Greek and Jew, circumcised and uncircumcised, barbarian, Scythian, slave and freeman, but Christ is all, and in all.

Paul's Response to the Roman World: Placing Paul in a Time Line

There is a distinct lack of detail on Messianism and the Messianic letters (Hebrews and James) outside of Acts 1-8. The new leader was added (1); Pentecost and the beginning shadow of the New Covenant began (2); The local ministry of Peter and John in Jerusalem was recorded (3-4), the challenge of truth in the Ananias and Sapphira story is unfolded (5), the testing and stoning of Stephen gave rise to the spread of the church (6-7), the moving ministry of Philip is recorded (8). Persecuting the church was a Tarsian Jew that God had big plans for!

Paul was likely **born about 4 or 5 CE**, the son of a Free Roman Jew of Tarsus (Acts 22:28).

Conversion 36 CE (Acts 9): Paul was saved near the age that a priest became consecrated (30) and about the age the Savior was at His Crucifixion. Half of Paul's life was already gone when he came to Christ. 2 Corinthians 11:32 records Paul's escape from Damascus shortly after his salvation (the basket and wall story). The calculation for this date is based on Josephus, who offers the detail that Aretas was king of Arabia between 36-39 CE, and Eusebius that tells us the events in Paul's life came shortly after Aretas ascended to the throne in 36 CE.

Three Years in Arabia (36/37 – 39/40; cp. Acts 9:23): Since Galatians includes the detail that Paul was three years in Arabia (or that it was three years total from his leaving to his return – cp. Galatians 1:15-18 with Acts 9:26 closes this description with a trip to Jerusalem). If Paul left Damascus in 36, the return to Jerusalem could be dated at 39. If it was later, the return may be as late as 40 CE.

First Mission Journey (45-47 CE, cp. Acts 13-14): The journey took place shortly after the death of Herod Agrippa I (44 CE according to dates established by Josephus Flavius Antiquities 19.8.2 – A festival to celebrate the ascension of Claudius to the Imperial role, cp. Acts 12). Since Sergius Paulus was the proconsul in Cyprus (it was a Senatorial province) only in the year 45 CE, the beginning date seems certain. Bear in mind the Roman year begins in March, so the current reckoning of time must be open to 46 CE as well. Paul was about 40 or 41 years of age in 45 CE, for the beginning of the journey.

The Jerusalem Council (50 CE, cp. Acts 15; Gal. 2:1-10): If the reference in Galatians 2:1 is to suggest that the council met fourteen years after the conversion of Paul, the date of the council would be 50 CE. Paul was about age 45 or 46 at that time.

The Second Mission Journey (51-54 CE, cp. Acts 15:36-18:22): Paul was about 46 or 47 years of age when he left on the second mission journey and finished the journey at about age 49 or 50. According to an inscription found in Delphi in 1908, Gallio was proconsul in Achaia in the year 51/52 (March to March). Gallio was at the bema in Corinth when Paul was brought there (cp. Acts. 18:12). Paul appeared to stay on until the next man took the office, dating the journey. Though Paul is rightly regarded in Church History as a great writer, his career in that regard began during the second journey, a mere seventeen or eighteen years before his death.

- **1 Thessalonians**
- **2 Thessalonians**

The Third Mission Journey (54-58 CE, cp. Acts 18:23-21:14): With very little break, Paul moved into the Third Mission Journey in his early 50's for the next three years. The ministry included a swift pass through what is now central modern Turkey toward the west coast of Asia Minor, for an extended stay in Ephesus (nearly three years). After establishing the work firmly in Asia Minor, Paul moved west to Macedonia and Greece, before returning along the Asian coast (Troas, Mytilene, Assos, Coos, Rhodos, etc. The mission ended back in Provincia Judea.

- **Galatians**
- **1 Corinthians**
- **2 Corinthians**
- **Romans**

Paul's Arrest in Jerusalem (58 or 59 CE, cp. Acts 21:17-23:32): Antoninus Felix was appointed under Claudius in 52 CE.

He married the Jewish princess Drusilla (daughter of Herod Agrippa 1, cp. Acts 24:24) as his third wife. At 15 years of age Drusilla was married to Azizus, King of Emesa (northern Syrian city of "Hims" today, but she left him for Felix. They had a son named Agrippa that died at Vesuvius in 79 CE. Felix's term overlapped that of Festus for a brief time in 58 CE. Felix was recalled to Rome to answer for disturbances and riots in Syria and Provincia Judea during his term. Since the overlapping dates of Felix and Festus's time in Provincia Judea are known, scholars feel comfortable dating Paul's arrest to about 58, and his incarceration in Caesarea to the time between 58-61 CE. Paul was arrested at about age 53 or 54, and journeyed to Rome at about age 57.

Journey to Rome (61 CE, cp. Acts 27:1-28:16): Festus died after a few years in office. No record of his work before taking office has been found. He was generally judged superior in administration to Felix in his brief leadership. Before he died, as recorded in Acts 25:12, Festus acceded to Paul's appeal to appear before Emperor Nero which resulted in Paul being deported from Caesarea, shortly after Festus sought help structuring the written appeal from Herod Agrippa II (Acts 25-26). Moved by ship at about 56 years of age to Rome (in 61 or 62 CE - Acts 27 and 28), Paul remained about two years under house arrest while awaiting an appearance before Caesar in the year 63 CE or 64 CE. Paul likely met Nero for his first hearing in the end of the year 61 CE (following William Ramsey's date) or perhaps in year 62 CE. He had been **staying at his own expense under guard in a small area close to the Tiber** (near or at San Paolo alla Regola in Rome) where tanners and dyers had their operations.

- **Ephesians**
- **Philippians**
- **Colossians**
- **Philemon**

Paul's Final Travels (62-65 CE, after the record of the Acts of the Apostles): It seems that while in Rome (or just after) in the year **62** CE, an earthquake (a subduction in the Bay of Naples) caused a tsunami with a tidal wave that swamped the ships at Ostia harbor near to Rome, ruining as much as one third of the Alexandrian grain. Coins were minted to show the people that all was well in spite of the disaster, but Nero must have found himself scrambling to meet the needs of the people for bread in that year. Paul was released to travel more between the years 62 and 65. There is much speculation about where he actually went, though it is *only* speculation.

Paul's Final Arrest and Death (65-67CE): Paul was arrested again (perhaps while traveling in Asia Minor at the behest of a bad report by Alexander the Coppersmith) and was held again in Rome, awaiting an audience with Emperor Nero. A general persecution was raised against the Christians by Nero, after 64 CE (because of the great fire of Rome), and Paul may have faced no other charges than being a part of a seditious group. Paul was eventually executed by beheading (according to early reports) in about 67 or 68 CE (at age of early 60's).

- **1 Timothy**
- **Titus**
- **2 Timothy**

Paul's Response to the Roman World:
Paul the Writer

Paul's major contribution to the work of the Gospel was much more than the founding of local churches – though that is no small task of itself. He was also a writer, and the Spirit-breathed Epistles are a treasure to the church of every age. In these Epistles, Paul used the sample problems of a local church to offer timeless truths and principles that are instructive for a whole range of ever-changing issues in the church.

Paul wrote the Epistles that we have in four groupings – four times in his life. He didn't begin until he was in his mid-forties, with the writings to Thessalonica during the perilous and turbulent times of the second mission journey. Note the four groups of writing as they are organized below.

Stage One: Prophetic -- During second mission journey between 51-54 CE when Paul was in his upper 40's. (Image: Shofar).

> **1 Thessalonians**: Personal and Biographical (relational) – Paul was worried and then relieved with Tim's report about them, (1-3); Instructional (three marks of distinction of a believer: Sexual Purity; Proper work life; Proper view of death and resurrection) – (4-5).

> **2 Thessalonians**: Inspiration to oppressed (notes to suffering followers (1), Instruction to perplexed (concerning faked writing and man of sin (2), Injunction to disorderly (face disorderly among you (3).

Stage Two: Polemic -- During third journey between 54-58 CE when Paul was in his lower 50's. (Image: Scalpel of a surgeon).

> **Romans**: Because you were condemned (1:1-3:20), and God justified you (3:21-5:21), empowered you to be distinct (6-8) and explained His plan to keep His promises to Abraham (9-11). It is right for you to submit

your life for Divine inspection (12:1-2), and live the life of a real believer (12:2-16:27).

1 Corinthians: I heard from the household of Chloe that you have misplaced your loyalty (men over message-1-4). It is commonly known you have misplaced values (love over truth-5) and misplaced standards (world over Word/body-6). Here are the answers to your questions concerning relationships and marriage (7), doubtful issues (8-10), symbols of your faith (11), gifts and serving together (12-14), resurrection (15) and financial stewardship (16).

2 Corinthians: There are three issues I wish to share with you - I am not with you and I need to **explain** (one key evidence of truth is transformation! 1-7), I still have an **expectation** of you (giving 8-9), and I need to **exhort** you to follow proper leadership (10-13)

*Galatians: You have left the formula of salvation in the Gospel, though it was not human in origin and fully confirmed by the leaders (1-2). The Spirit came through the Gospel without the Law (showing it unnecessary to salvation) and you are bending the purpose of the Atonement Law that has been amended, going backward in faith. Stop! (3-4). Move ahead by faith alone, but walk in the Spirit and not by the flesh, caring for one another.

Stage Three: Philosophical – During house arrest in 61-63 CE when Paul was near 60. (Image: Square of a builder).

Ephesians: Gentile believers are not second class citizens of the Kingdom. Call (1-3), Conduct (4:1-6:9), Conflict (6:10-20). They were called to a Divine heritage (1) by Divine initiative (2) for a Divine purpose (3), their conduct should follow five "walks" (4:1-6-9) and the must suit up for conflict (6:10-20).

Philippians: Apostle's Desire (Prayer 1:1-11), Apostle's Diagnosis (Three Ailments 1:12-4:9. Paul saw three problems: Need to identify God's hand at work (1:12-30); Need to use knowledge given by God to set priorities

(2:1-30); Need to face that wrong priorities bring wrong fruit (3:1-4:9).), Apostle's demonstration (Model, 4:10-23).

Colossians: God called the believer with certain goals of life transformation (1:1-12). He has the Divine right to anticipate our obedience (1:13-29). The practical surrender works out in daily choices of obedience, as well as strict defining of my identity in Jesus and His work (2:1-23) brought on by a complete change in the focus of my everyday life (3:1-4:6).

Philemon: Ten steps to repair a breach between two believers.

Stage Four: Pastoral – Between imprisonments about 63-68 CE when Paul was in his low to mid 60's. (Image: Staff of a Shepherd).

1 Timothy: Timothy needed encouragement to focus on his personal leadership and the work of the body by understanding the process and goals of working with other believers (1). He needed to understand and instruct on proper behaviors in the believers (2), as well as identify proper leadership priorities and practices (3). He needed to move the flock through perils (4) while fostering godly relationships and avoiding common enemy traps (5). Finally, he needed to practice godliness in daily life (6).

Titus: The letter outlines six major principles to establishing well-grounded and God-pleasing churches: Choose leadership **wisely**! (1:5-9); **protect the truth entrusted to you**! (1:10-16); Train a group to become a true church in equipment and functions! (2:1-10); **keep working** with those formed by grace and maintained by obedience in expectation of the Lord's return,! (2:11-15); **be gracious** toward the world and its leaders – a humility bathed in memory! (3:1-7), **Be careful** not to ignore error and contention! (3:8-11).

2 Timothy: To face the changes ahead, Timothy needed to change his thinking (1) and be reassured that victory came from obedience, not schemes of men (2). In spite of the battle, he needed the encouragement that he could see through the darkness with the Word (3) and navigate the dangers that were quickly coming upon him (4).

These four "seasons" of Paul's life were used by God to communicate truth to the church of both the first century and every century since. Any story of Paul's life, must take into consideration the events surrounding the writings of each Epistle, and for most of them we have the advantage of the Book of Acts to fill in the detail of these events.

*Galatians: the date of this letter is uncertain. I suspect it was quite early after the Jerusalem Council decision of Acts 15.

Paul's Response to the Roman World: Paul and Nero – A Collision Course

Paul lived and traveled under five Imperial rulers in his life – Augustus (23 BCE-14 CE), Tiberius (14-37 CE), Caligula (37-41 CE), Claudius (41-54 CE) and Nero (54-68 CE). Augustus, Tiberius and Caligula were *Princeps* during Paul's unregenerate life, and neither seemed to care much of the beginnings of the Christian movement. Emperor Claudius apparently expelled the Jews from Rome because of unrest evoked by Christians: **"Since the Jews constantly made disturbances at the instigation of Chrestus, he [Emperor Claudius] expelled them from Rome"** (Suetonius, Life of Claudius, 25:4; Acts 18:2). Officially, Emperor Claudius died at around noon on 13 October 54. Unofficially, he died during the preceding night or just before dawn. The "missing" hours were needed for Agrippina, after having a significant hand in her husband's death, to make the proper arrangements for the smooth transition of power. Initially, Agrippina made little effort to conceal her expectations control. She had several enemies openly killed, and was even found on coinage.

Though the first years of Nero's reign (54–59) were widely **regarded as excellent**, the accession of Nero as the fifth "princeps" in 54 saw a young and inexperienced prince elevated to the most powerful office in the world, and it was a recipe for disaster. Nero initially did quite well, in particular because of the influence of advisors **Seneca**, Nero's tutor and **Burrus**, the Praetorian prefect, who held his vices in check. He ruled with reason and moderation on the surface. Behind the scenes, there were worrying indications as Nero chafed against the influence of his mother (who placed his counselors around him). As he grew into the role, he showed less and less interest in mundane administration, but treasured writing poetry and pursuing music, and the thrill of gaming. Agrippina (his mother) did not like what she saw. What she didn't see was his deep drives in sexual vices.

Nero, at one point early fell in love with a freedwoman named **Acte** (55 CE). Seneca and Burrus tolerated the affair, but **Agrippina was appalled**. Agrippina publicly upbraided her son for his feelings, and began to extol the virtues of Britannicus (a possible rival to the throne). Nero had Britannicus poisoned and his mother removed to her own house, and her imperial guard was withdrawn. She faded from the coinage of Rome from that time. The next we hear of her is in the writings of Tacitus in the year 59. By the year 59 CE, Paul was awaiting trial in Caesarea, and that year marked a turning point in Nero's reign for three reasons:

- First, he **performed on stage** for the first time. Nero had been devoting himself to playing the lyre, singing, acting, and composing poetry. To put Nero's desire to perform in perspective, we must appreciate the fact that stage performers usually came from the lower orders. The Roman aristocracy found them repellent. He knew his mother would never approve of such behavior.

- Second, he **fell in love** with Poppaea Sabina (of Pompeii): a beautiful woman that was in her second marriage when Nero and her rendezvoused in love (She was married to the Roman general Otho). She was later to die, likely being kicked to death while pregnant by Nero himself, if Suetonius is to be believed.

- Third, **he killed his own mother**. An ex-slave called Anicetus built a collapsible boat to make the murder look like a maritime accident. When she survived, Nero dispatched with a column of troops, who surrounded the villa, and Agrippina was then hacked to death by her son's soldiers.

In 59 and, Nero **indulged a fantasy** and donned racing chariots, an even newer low for the Roman princeps. His lyre-playing and singing annoyed the social upper classes. By 60, Nero staged the "Neronia" (humbly named after the sponsor!): a literary, musical, gymnastic, and equestrian competition modeled on Greek spectacles.

Paul likely met Nero for his first hearing in the end of the year 61 CE (following William Ramsey's date). He had been staying at his own expense under guard in a small area close to the Tiber where tanners and dyers had their operations. He lived in modest chambers and offered us letters like Ephesians,

Philippians, Colossians and Philemon. Particularly in **Philippians**, one can **see the hope of the future**, as Paul felt optimistic that he could explain his faith in non-threatening terms to the state. He wrote to the Philippians toward the end of his house arrest, anticipating the trial with confidence:

Phil 1:12 "Now I want you to know, brethren, that my circumstances have turned out for the greater progress of the gospel, 13 so that my imprisonment in the cause of Christ has become well known throughout the whole praetorian guard and to everyone else, 14 and that most of the brethren, trusting in the Lord because of my imprisonment, have far more courage to speak the word of God without fear."

In essence, the charge made against him regarded an issue for Jewish courts – the violation of a barrier in the Temple past which he was accused of taking a non-Jew. It was not a capital crime, and Paul felt he could argue effectively. Dr. Luke apparently volunteered to come along with Paul in his transport, which implies openly that he traveled as his slave to Rome in Acts 28 (or would not have been afforded the opportunity). He suffered the shipwreck on the way, but offered the confidence and hope Paul needed on cold nights facing his trial. During the time of his house arrest, Paul seems to have sent his companions on deliveries (Luke may have carried Philippians, while Aristarchus and Epaphrus were sent back toward Asia Minor). Demas was with him, but Paul had doubts about his reliability. The last part of his time in Rome he was mostly alone, but he was soon released and began to travel again.

While in Rome in the year **62** CE, an **earthquake** (subduction in the Bay of Naples) caused a tsunami with a tidal wave that swamped the ships at Ostia harbor near to Rome, ruining as much as one third of the Alexandrian grain. Coins were minted to show the people that all was well in spite of the disaster, but Nero must have found himself scrambling to meet the needs of the people for bread in that year.

Paul was released **to travel more between the years 62 and 65**. After he departed Rome, it appears that he went to **Crete** (2 Tim. 4:17) with Timothy and Titus, leaving Titus to organize the church there. He and Timothy headed to **Macedonia** (1 Tim. 1:13) and over to **Ephesus**, where Paul excommunicated to trouble makers (Hymenaeus and Alexander, 1 Tim. 1:20) and left Timothy to work on the restoration of the believers there. Back to **Macedonia** he went, issuing letters to both Titus in Crete and Timothy in Ephesus. Traveling back to Asia Minor, Alexander the metalworker aided men in arresting Paul at **Troas** (2 Tim. 4:20). He was transferred to **Miletos** and back to Rome via ship. This time, the mood had changed.

During Paul's travels in 64 CE, Nero raced chariots in public at Naples. These games helped to bring hope back to the region, still dealing with the blow of the earthquake two years earlier. Many public works were under repair. By mid-July of 64, the **fire of Rome** started in shops near the Circus Maximus, devastating the surrounding hills as people poured into the narrow streets and were suffocated, crushed, or roasted alive in their flight. Nero was at his estate at Antium on the coast and returned to the city, opening public buildings to refugees, offering food and supplies Ten days after the fire, it was obvious the devastation was **massive**.

Nero singled out the strange eastern cultists called Christians as the problem. Rome basically allowed religious traditions to coexist unless they threatened the public order or cross purposed with Roman interests. Since failure to perform the required rituals risked the wrath of the gods, (seen in fires, floods, etc.) Christians seemed likely culprits. They disapproved of the rituals that were so vital to the welfare of the community and upset the social order by refusing to recognize rank in their membership.

Paul may have arrived back in Rome as early as **66**, but Nero was gone for a year in **Greece** to compete in the Greek festivals, where he (shockingly) won every game (including ones he never participated in!). **Nero returned to Rome late in 67**, but continued to act, sing, recite poetry, and race in public – where our sources reflect that the elite felt that Nero's artistic performances were the height of irresponsibility. Though the Emperor returned in an exceptional mood, the **palace and the Senate's tenor quickly collapsed his mood to one of darkness**. In that state, Paul knew he stood virtually no chance.

More than that, it appears Paul sensed his time was near. 2 Timothy was his response to the realization that he wasn't going to be on the earth much longer.

(For a great discussion on these times, check out St. Paul: Traveler and Roman Citizen by William Ramsey as well as the lectures of Dr. Garrett Fagan. Both are excellent and rewarding for the research.)

Paul's Response to the Roman World:
Paul and His Companions

The Book of Acts and the Epistles of Paul mention a number of characters that enter the scene with little explanation and no real attempt at explanation of their role. This chapter is a **helpful reference tool** to "check in" on as you are reading through the Biblical text. For the sake of ease, the people are arranged alphabetically. The list is not exhaustive, but is comprehensive enough to help most Bible students and travelers to Bible lands to get a better sketch of those mentioned in the ancient narratives. It is intended as a reference, so you can skip reading this chapter and simply refer back to it as you are studying and come upon a name in the text of the New Testament.

Agabus: Agabus may be one of the seventy disciples mentioned in Luke 10:1, 17. He traveled from Jerusalem to visit the church at Antioch and there prophesied regarding an approaching famine (Acts 11:27-28), a prophecy that prompted a special offering for the Judean believers (Acts 11:29-30). Then, years later, Agabus met Paul in Caesarea at the end of his Third Journey and warned him of the troubles and imprisonment that awaited him in Jerusalem. On this occasion, Agabus went so far as to remove Paul's belt and used it to act out his coming bondage! (Acts 21:10-11).

Alexander of Ephesus: Alexander was a man of Ephesus who was put forward by his fellow Jews to try to calm the riot there, an uproar started by Demetrius the silversmith in reaction to Paul's preaching (Acts 19:23-41). Alexander "beckoned with the hand" to the mob in the theater, but to no avail; seeing he was a Jew, the crowd refused to let him speak. The Jews "putting him forward" to speak on their behalf may have been an attempt to dissociate themselves from Paul and his message and to show that they had no sympathy with him. [An apostate mentioned in 1 Tim. 1:20 who "made shipwreck" of his faith may or may not be the same individual. Likewise, with the coppersmith in 2 Timothy 4:14 who did Paul "much evil."]

Ananias of Damascus: Following Paul's blinding conversion on the road to Damascus, his fellow travelers led him by the hand into that city, to the house of one Judas where Paul ate and drank nothing for three days (Acts 9:3-9). Then Ananias, a member of the Judeo-Christian community in Damascus and well aware of Paul's persecution of the church, received a vision directing him to go find Paul at the house of Judas in "Straight Street." Worth noting are Ananias' initial openness and willingness to hear (9:10) and then his very human reaction as he raises objections based on Paul's notoriety (9:13-14). It is likely also that Ananias had good reason to be wary of Judas' house, since it is likely Paul's fellow travelers—persecutors of the church—had simply delivered him to a sympathetic refuge or lodging previously known to them. Regardless, Ananias obediently went to find Paul and minister to him, first imparting the Holy Spirit to him and restoring his sight through the laying-on of hands, and then baptizing him (9:10-19). [Note: The Damascus street called "Straight" is identified with the modern "street of bazaars," where a so-called "house of Judas" is still pointed out to visitors.]

Apollos of Alexandria: Apollos first appears in the Acts narrative as an eloquent speaker who arrives in Ephesus ca. 49 CE and begins preaching in the synagogue there. He was well versed in the scriptures and had learned much about Jesus, but he knew "only the Baptism of John." (In this, he may have influenced the disciples Paul encountered later in Acts 19:1-3.) When the Christian leaders Aquila and Priscilla took notice of Apollos and found his teaching lacking, they gave him further instruction in the faith and then encouraged his continued ministry. Settling in Corinth, Apollos became an influential leader in that church and also became acquainted with the Apostle Paul. It is clear from First Corinthians that Apollos came to be admired by some Corinthian Christians as a greater authority than Paul, perhaps because of his oratorical skills. Paul likely has this in mind when he reminds them that he (Paul) came "*not with excellency of speech*" or "*enticing words*" (1 Cor. 2:1-4), thus urging the Corinthians to focus on the simple *message* of the gospel, without regard to style or personalities. Because it is the Corinthian *believers* that Paul rebukes—not Apollos—for creating and fostering these divisions, it appears Apollos himself did nothing to encourage the factionalism.

Aquila: Aquila and his wife Priscilla—always mentioned together—were Jewish followers of Jesus in Corinth, where they offered Paul lodging in their home and became fellow-workers with him, both in the trade of tent-making and in spreading the gospel of Christ (Acts 18:1-3). The couple had settled in Corinth after being expelled from Rome, victims of the edict of Claudius against the Jews in 49/50 CE. That they were owners of property and able to travel widely suggests they had considerable financial means. Aquila and Priscilla, after encountering Paul in Corinth, traveled with him as far as Ephesus, where they lived and apparently hosted a house-church for the believers. There they also met the Christian preacher Apollos, whom they gently taught and corrected when they found his message lacking (Acts 18:26). Aquila and Priscilla apparently later returned to Rome (after the edict was lifted in 54 CE) and became prominent in the Christian community there as well (Rom. 16:3). As supporters of Paul—to the point of putting themselves in danger (Rom. 16:3-4)—and as leaders in the various churches, this couple's value to the apostle is reflected in the frequent greetings addressed to them in Paul's letters.

Aristarchus the Macedonian: Aristarchus appears as one of two travelling companions of Paul dragged into the theater at Ephesus during the riot in that city (Acts 19:29), an incident that takes place on the outbound leg of the 3rd missionary journey. On the return leg the same journey (Paul's last trip to Jerusalem, ca. 55 CE), Aristarchus is one of at least seven men accompanying Paul as his party crosses from Europe into Asia. He is one of two mentioned from the Macedonian city of Thessalonica, the other being Secundus. These companions may have been helping Paul gather money from the Gentile churches as a contribution to the poor in Jerusalem (2 Cor. 8:1—9:5). An Aristarchus, probably the same individual, is identified in Col. 4:10-11 as a Jewish convert, and as such he would have shared Paul's desire to reach Jerusalem in time for the great pilgrim festival of Pentecost (Shavuot) (Acts 20:16). Aristarchus appears once again accompanying Paul as the latter embarks from Caesarea on his voyage to Rome as a prisoner (Acts 27:2). It is probably the same person mentioned in passing in Philemon 24.

Barnabas of Cyprus (Joses): Barnabas, born on the island of Cyprus of Jewish parents of the tribe of Levi, perhaps came to Jerusalem because of his priestly connections (some have surmised he was a fellow-student with Paul of the sage Gamaliel). A cousin of John Mark, he became a leader in the Jerusalem church and was given the nickname Barnabas by the apostles (Acts 4:36-37). When Jerusalem's early Judeo-Christian community "had all things common" (Acts 4:32-35), Barnabas sold a piece of property and turned the proceeds over to the apostles. When Saul, after his conversion, found the Jerusalem believers suspicious of his motives, Barnabas took him and introduced him to the apostles (Acts 9:26-27). Sent by the Jerusalem church to supervise the burgeoning Christian work at Antioch, Barnabas found the enterprise so demanding that he brought Saul from Tarsus to help him, and the two labored together in Antioch for a year (Acts 11:22-26). Barnabas and Paul were then sent up to Jerusalem by the Antioch church to deliver a special famine offering (11:27-30), and on their return they brought John Mark with them down to Antioch (12:25). After being commissioned as missionaries by the believers there, the two men, with John Mark, set out on the first missionary journey (13:2-3). This tour (ca. 46-48 CE)—in the course of which John Mark left and returned to Jerusalem—took Barnabas and Paul to Cyprus and the principal cities of Iconium in southeastern Asia Minor (13:4—14:26). Barnabas and Paul then attended the council in Jerusalem, where the proper relationship of Gentile believers to Jewish ritual law was debated (15:1-4), and afterward they and others delivered the resulting letter of instruction to Antioch. There Barnabas and Paul, before the apostle's 2nd missionary journey, sharply disagreed about the future role of John Mark in their joint ministry and as a result parted ways, Barnabas taking John Mark into Cyprus and Paul setting out with Silas through Asia Minor toward Greece (Acts 15:25-41).

Crispus of Corinth: Crispus, chief ruler of the synagogue at Corinth, placed his faith in Christ through the ministry of Paul, along with his whole family (Acts 18:8). Crispus is later specified as one baptized by Paul personally, apparently an uncommon occurrence (1 Cor. 1:14). His conversion shows that the Corinthian church was not entirely Gentile.

Damaris of Athens: Damaris was a woman of Athens who, in response to Paul's preaching there, became one of his few converts in that city.

Dionysius the Areopagite: Only in Acts 17:34 is the individual Dionysius mentioned, along with the fact that he and others became believers in response to Paul's preaching before the Areopagus of Athens. Beyond this, anything else we might surmise about him lies in his designation as an "Areopagite." The word Areopagus denotes both a place and an institution in ancient Athens. The Greek term in Acts 17 (vss. 19 and 22) is *Areios Pagos* ("martial peak"), the name of a low hill lying northwest of the Acropolis and near the Parthenon. This rocky prominence was associated with the god of war, *Ares* in Greek and "Mars" in Latin (hence, the KJV rendering "Mars Hill" in vs. 22). The Latinized form of the Greek words is "Areopagus." The council that met there—and assumed the name—had originated in Greece's golden age as a body of advisors to the Athenian kings and in later centuries functioned as a judicial body. However, by the 1st century CE the Areopagus had come to have a different role. Probably assembled on stone seats, meeting in the open air, their job was to exercise control over all those who wished to lecture or teach in Athens. The man Dionysius, then, as a member of the Areopagus, is presumed to be an influential civic leader, highly educated, and one intimately familiar with all manner of philosophical and religious discourse. Moreover, the group to which he belonged—in effect a collective "dean of faculty" for Athens' philosophical community—would have had a special interest in any teaching regarded as "new" and "strange," as the gospel promulgated by Paul certainly was (Acts 17:19-21).

Erastus: Paul, during an extended stay in Ephesus on the outbound leg of his 3rd missionary journey, sent Erastus and Timothy ahead of him into Macedonia (Acts 19:22). Beyond this, nothing else is known for certain from the Bible about this particular Erastus. Later, when Paul passes through Macedonia and into Asia Minor on the return leg of the same journey, Erastus is not among those listed as travelling with him (Acts 20:1-4). [Notes: The Erastus of Acts 19:22 is often regarded as the same as that mentioned in 2 Tim. 4:20, an associate of Paul's who stayed in Corinth, a common link between the two being Timothy. Probably neither of the aforementioned individuals, however, is to be equated with the Erastus appearing in the greetings of Rom. 16:23. That Erastus, presumably a Christian convert, held a position of some importance as a city treasurer—probably of Corinth, since Paul's letter to the Romans is usually regarded to have been written from there. (This latter Erastus is very probably the subject of an inscription unearthed in the ruins of ancient Corinth: "Erastus built this plaza in appreciation for receiving a public office, and he used his own money, not town money.")]

Eutychus of Troas: On the return leg of his 3rd missionary journey (ca. 55 CE), Paul spent a week in Troas, a city on the Aegean coast at the northwestern tip of Asia Minor. There Paul delivered a discourse to a group of believers gathered in a third story room and one of them, Eutychus, perched on a windowsill, fell into a deep sleep. The text gives ample reason for Eutychus' slumber: the disciples had just had a meal, having come together to "break bread;" there were "many lights" (i.e., oil lamps) in the room—throwing off heat and consuming oxygen – while Paul was "long preaching" far into the evening (Acts 20:7-9). At length, Eutychus tumbled out the window, fell to the ground, and was found dead by those who rush to his aid. Paul, however, bent over the young man, embraced him, and restored him to life (Acts 20:9-10).

Gaius of Derbe: Gaius of Derbe is mentioned as one of several believers traveling with Paul as the apostle crosses from Macedonia into Asia Minor, on the return leg of his 3rd missionary journey. [Gaius was a common masculine name in NT times, and this Gaius (of Derbe) is probably not to be identified with other individuals of the same name: Paul's host at Corinth when he wrote his Epistle to the Romans (Rom. 16:23) and who was baptized by Paul (1 Cor. 1:14); a Macedonian, a traveling companion of Paul caught up in the riot at Ephesus (Acts 19:29); and an otherwise unknown recipient of the Third Epistle of John (vs. 1).]

Gaius of Macedonia: Gaius appears, along with Aristarchus, as a travelling companion of Paul in Ephesus, on the outbound leg of the apostle's 3rd missionary journey, ca. 53—55 CE. The two men were seized and dragged into the theater at Ephesus, during the riot in that city (Acts 19:29), when the mob was unable to find Paul himself. [Gaius was a common masculine name in NT times, and this Gaius (of Macedonia) is probably not to be identified with other individuals of the same name: Paul's host at Corinth when he wrote his Epistle to the Romans (Rom. 16:23) and who was baptized by Paul (1 Cor. 1:14); a man of Derbe in Asia Minor, a traveling companion of Paul (Acts 20:4); and a recipient of the Third Epistle of John (vs. 1).]

James the Just: James is named among the "brothers" of Jesus in parallel accounts in Matthew and Mark, and in Gal. 1:19 is called "the Lord's brother." While his actual familial relationship to Jesus is much debated, James is often regarded as an older half-brother of Jesus (the Greek "adelphos" is usually rendered "brother" but can indicate more distant relations, even a cousin). This is based in part on Roman Catholic dogma which holds that Mary, the mother of Jesus, bore no other children. An argument—a cultural one—is also made from the incident of Jesus entrusting to John (a non-relative) the care of his mother, a request which makes more sense if Jesus has no full siblings. While the Gospels reflect no special role for James in Jesus' earthly ministry, he is identified as one to whom Jesus appeared after his resurrection (1 Cor.15:7). Then the Lord's "brothers" are found with the apostles after his ascension (Acts 1:14). James met with Saul (Paul) ca. 37 CE, when that apostle made his first trip to Jerusalem following his conversion (Acts 9:27; Gal. 1:19). In Acts 12:17, Peter leaves a message for James and the other apostles at the house of Mary regarding his miraculous escape from prison. In Acts 15 James has emerged as the central figure of the Jerusalem church, recognized successor to the leadership role originally exercised by Peter and "the twelve." There James presides at a council (ca. 50/51 CE) debating to what degree Gentile Christians are subject to the Mosaic law (Acts 15:1-29; Gal. 2:9), and it is he who renders a formal decision (15:13, 19) which is then circulated abroad in a letter of instruction (15:22ff). James is last mentioned in the Acts narrative when Paul makes his final visit to Jerusalem, ca. 58 CE. First hearing Paul's report and rejoicing over his ministry, James and the others then warn him of the opposition against him stirred up by his enemies (Acts 21:17-27). Tradition says that James' death came only a few years later, at the hands of Jerusalem's priestly leadership (see above).

Jason of Thessalonica: Jason lived in Thessalonica (modern Thessaloniki), on the Aegean coast of Macedonia, and was the host of Paul and Silas when they visited that city to establish a Christian community there. In reaction to Paul's missionary work, the Jews fomented a riot and assaulted Jason's house, intending to seize Paul. Failing to find him, they instead brought out Jason and others and dragged them before the rulers of the city. There, as Paul's patron, Jason was required to give "security," i.e. accept legal responsibility for Paul's future activity (Acts 17:5-9). Jason (assuming it is the same one) is identified as a relative of Paul's and accompanied him from Thessalonica to Corinth (where the letter to the Romans was written) (Rom. 16:21).

John: Mark: John Mark was the son of Mary of Jerusalem, an early believer who opened her home as a gathering place for Jerusalem's primitive Judeo-Christian community (Acts 12:12ff). It was to this house, where he was already well-known, that Peter came following his miraculous release from prison, and it is not unlikely that he influenced the young John Mark in the faith (cp. "Marcus my son" in 1 Pet. 5:13). John Mark was apparently either the nephew or a cousin of Barnabas (Col. 4:10), and Barnabas and Paul, after delivering an offering to Jerusalem from the believers in Antioch, brought John Mark with them on their return (Acts 11:29-30; 12:25). John Mark then accompanied Paul and Barnabas on their first missionary journey. With the two he traveled across the island of Cyprus, but for unknown reasons parted from them at Perga on the southern coast of Asia Minor and from there returned to Jerusalem (Acts 13:5, 13). Back in Antioch, ca. 48-49 CE, a sharp disagreement arose between Paul and Barnabas over John Mark's future role, Paul deeply concerned over the young man's previous abandonment of their work but Barnabas determined to take his young relative with them again. As a result, Barnabas and Paul parted company, Barnabas taking Mark with him for further ministry in Cyprus, and Paul setting out with Silas on the second missionary journey (Acts 15:36-41). That both Paul and Peter later valued John Mark, as a fellow-worker and probably as a companion in Rome, is clear from passing references in their epistles (Col. 4:10; Philemon 24; 1 Pet. 5:13)—assuming they are all references to the same individual. A Mark is present with Timothy at Ephesus as well (2 Tim. 4:11). Mark (Marcos/Marcus) was so common a name in the Roman world that these identifications, and even the traditional attribution of the Gospel of Mark to this individual, cannot be made with certainty.

John the Apostle: John was likely one of the two followers of John the Baptist who heard Jesus proclaimed "the Lamb of God" and began following him (Jn. 1:35-40). Of the two, one was Andrew and the other is conspicuous by not being named, as is the case with John elsewhere in the Gospel bearing his name. If true, this early association of John with Andrew lends itself to the tradition that John was from Bethsaida, the city of Andrew and Peter (Jn. 1:44). John's more direct and formal call comes in the context of fishing with others on the Sea of Galilee (Matt. 4:21-22). From Jesus, John and James received the nickname "Boanerges" or "Sons of Thunder" (Mk. 3:17). If this denotes, as often suggested, an impulsive, tempestuous disposition, it is perfectly illustrated by their proposal to call fire down from heaven upon an unreceptive Samaritan village (Lk. 9:54). John and James also held a place of prominence among the disciples, perhaps reflected in their mother's bold request that her sons receive places of special honor in Jesus' coming Kingdom (Mt. 20:20-23). As a member of Jesus' close inner circle, along with James and Peter, John was a witness of Jesus' Transfiguration (Mark 9:2). With Peter he helped prepare the final Passover meal in Jerusalem (Lk. 22:8) and then reclined next to Jesus at the table (Jn. 13:23). And at Gethsemane, Jesus took the three apart, revealed His special burden, and asked them to "watch" with Him while He prayed (Mt. 26:36-38). Of "the twelve," John alone was noted to have presence at the Crucifixion, where Jesus entrusted to him the care of His mother (Jn. 19:26-27). Later, hearing Mary Magdalene's report of Jesus' Resurrection, John raced with Peter to the empty tomb (Jn. 20:1-8). A witness of Jesus' post-resurrection appearances and ascension, John became an important leader of Jerusalem's primitive Christian community and was called a "pillar" of that church by Paul (Gal. 2:6-10). Galatians 1:13—2:9 suggested that John was still present in Jerusalem in the late 40s CE, but church tradition later places him at Ephesus, perhaps with Mary, Jesus' mother. After his exile to Patmos during the reign of Domitian, John probably returned to Ephesus and died there ca. 100 CE.

Judas Barsabas: This man was a trusted disciple sent by the apostles in Jerusalem to accompany Paul, Barnabas, and Silas in delivering a letter of instruction to the believers at Antioch (Acts 15:22). Variant teachings had arisen concerning the proper relationship of Gentile believers to the Jewish ritual law, i.e., what demands were to be placed upon them, especially with regard to circumcision. In response, the apostles had convened a conference in Jerusalem to discuss and decide upon the matter. The resulting letter (intended for believers in Antioch, Syria and Cilicia) freed Gentile Christians (with the exception of certain proscriptions) from the burden of observing the Mosaic law (Acts 15:1-21). In Antioch, Judas' role was to verbally affirm the content of the written apostolic decree (vs. 27), in the course of which he "exhorted the brethren...and confirmed them" (vs. 32). Judas was then released to return to Jerusalem, but the others remained to carry out further ministry in Antioch (Acts 15:33-35).

Judas of Damascus: Following Paul's blinding conversion on the road leading from Jerusalem to Damascus, his fellow-travelers—presumably Jews likewise bent on persecuting the believers there (Acts 9:1-2)—led him by the hand into Damascus. The place Paul was taken was the house of Judas, probably a refuge or lodging previously known to them, where the still-blinded Paul ate and drank nothing for three days (9:3-9). Then Ananias, a Damascus believer, made his way to Judas' house in "the street which is called Straight," in response to a vision. At Judas' house, Ananias ministered to Paul and through the laying-on of hands, restored his sight and imparted the Holy Spirit (9:10-19). [Note: The Damascus street called "Straight" is identified with the modern "street of bazaars," where a so-called "house of Judas" is still pointed out to visitors.]

Justus (Titias Justus): Justus is known only from the passing reference in Acts 18:7. After Paul preached to the Corinthian Jews and became the object of their wrath, he symbolically "shook his raiment" and proclaimed "from henceforth I will go unto the Gentiles" (Acts 18:5-6). Indeed, in the very next verse

Paul goes to a Gentile, being received into the house of Justus next door to a synagogue. (That there was more than one synagogue in Corinth is presumed from Acts 18, verses 8 and 17, where two individuals, Crispus and Sosthenes, both have the same title, "chief ruler of the synagogue.") That Justus was a "worshiper of God" probably means that he was a Gentile attracted to Judaism, perhaps holding among the Jews a kind of "associate" status. Whether intended or not, Justus serves as an effective metaphor for what is occurring in the narrative: As Paul turns from the Jews, he enters the house of a "just" Gentile who is close to Judaism—just as his house is "joined hard" to the synagogue.

Lucius of Cyrene: Lucius held a role as a special minister in the church of Antioch (Syrian Antioch, to distinguish from the one in Psidia in Asia Minor). He was among those who, at the prompting of the Holy Spirit, set apart Barnabas and Saul for a special work, ordained them with the laying on of hands, and sent them out (Acts 13:1). The designation that Lucius was "of Cyrene" most likely points to his family's origins in that city on the North African coast (modern-day Libya); it does not necessarily mean that he was born there. Before 300 BCE Cyrene had a thriving Jewish community and Cyrenian Jews are known to have migrated from there throughout the Mediterranean world. In Jerusalem, for example, there was a permanent community of Cyrenian Jews large enough to have their own synagogue (Acts 6:9). It is likewise clear that some of Jerusalem's Cyrenian Jews became believers in Jesus and, of these, some fled Jerusalem when a persecution broke out in connection with Stephen. When some of these believers— Hellenized Judeo-Christians—came to Antioch and "spoke to the Greeks" (Acts 11:20), it is not unreasonable to imagine Lucius among them. Finally, Romans 16:21 names a Lucius among Paul's associates and "kinsmen" (probably in the sense of fellow-Jews, not relatives) who are sending their greetings, but whether this is the same individual is unknown.

Luke: (Dr. Luke, or Luke the Evangelist): Writer of both a canonical Gospel of Jesus Christ and the Book of the Acts of the Risen Lord through His Apostles, Luke was perhaps a native of Antioch in Syria, and was thought to have been trained in Macedonia in medicine. The early church fathers ascribed to him authorship of a single literary work now divided between the Gospel and Acts. Later historians like Jerome and Eusebius validated the belief that was largely unchallenged until modernity. Luke appears in the Christian Scriptures as a medical doctor (Colossians 4), and a traveling companion of Paul. He is believed to have died a martyr, although accounts of the events do vary. Luke is mentioned in Paul's Epistle to Philemon, (1:24) as well as in Colossians 4:14 and 2 Timothy 4:11. The first person plural "we" sections of the Book of Acts suggest that he began his journeys with Paul in Macedonia – and may have been the man in Paul's "Macedonian Man" vision. Luke was again highlighted in the Anti-Marcionite Prologue to the Gospel of Luke, (either C2 CE or C4 CE). Epiphanius stated the Luke was one of the Seventy (Panarion 51.11), and John Chrysostom indicates at one point that the "brother" Paul mentioned in 2 Corinthians 8:18 was either Luke or Barnabas. As author of the Gospel bearing his name, he excluded himself from those who were eyewitnesses to Jesus' ministry, but he repeatedly used the word "we" in describing the Pauline missions in Acts of the Apostles, indicating that he was personally there at those times. The composition of both writings, indicate that the author was an educated man. The mention in Colossians apparently differentiating Luke from his colleagues "of the circumcision" has caused many to speculate that this indicates Luke was a Gentile. Luke's presence in Rome with the Apostle Paul near Paul's execution was attested in 2 Timothy 4:11: "Only Luke is with me." In addition, the account of the journey to Rome earlier in Paul's life was in the first person (affirming Luke's presence in Rome including Acts 28:16: "And when we came to Rome..."). The picture of Luke's life after Paul is muddled, but traditions place him in Boetia at death, with body relics shared between Padua (Santa Giustina reportedly has the body), Thebes (reportedly has a rib) and St. Vitus in Prague reportedly has his head). Archaeologist Sir William Ramsay wrote that "Luke is a historian of the first rank; not merely are his statements of fact trustworthy... [he] should be placed along with the very greatest of historians."

Lydia: Lydia was a businesswoman and "worshiper of God" from Thyatira in Asia Minor. On Paul's second missionary journey (49-52 CE), he and Silas came to the Macedonian coastal city of Philippi where, among a group of women praying by a riverside on the Jewish Sabbath, they encountered Lydia. Hearing the disciples words, Lydia believed, becoming the first Christian convert in Europe (16:14). After being baptized along with her whole household, Lydia offered Paul and Silas (and presumably Luke, the narrator of Acts 16) lodging in her house (16:15). After Paul and Silas were imprisoned in Philippi and finally released, they again went to Lydia's home, which by then seems to have become a center of Christian activity in the city (16:40). That Lydia was wealthy is inferred from her livelihood of selling expensive purple cloth (made with a precious dye derived in minute quantities from a particular marine snail, the Murex) and from her ability to offer extended lodging to Paul and his party. Some have characterized Lydia as a travelling businesswoman since, though Acts 16 places her in Philippi, she was "of Thyatira," and also because she is not mentioned later in Paul's epistle to the Philippians. Lydia's description as someone who "worshipped God" suggests she was a Gentile, either a proselyte or someone otherwise attracted to Judaism and holding a kind of "associate" status among the Jews (a "God-fearer"?). The fact that a riverside place of prayer is where Lydia joined others (not a synagogue) may point to a weak Jewish community in Philippi, without enough Jews to form a synagogue service (a minyan).

Manaen: Manaen held a role as a special minister in the church of Antioch (Syrian Antioch, to distinguish from the one in Psidia in Asia Minor). He was among those who, at the prompting of the Holy Spirit, set apart Barnabas and Saul for a special work, ordained them with the laying on of hands, and sent them out (Acts 13:1). We know nothing more of Manaen except that he "had been brought up with Herod the tetrarch" (i.e. Herod Antipas, ruler over Galilee from 4 BCE to 39 CE). The Greek word here, syntrophos is probably best rendered "foster brother," a designation given to boys of the same age as royal children with whom they were raised. (It is worth noting that Antipas, with his brother Archelaus, was educated at Rome.) This suggests that Manaen had been an intimate friend of Herod Antipas, or perhaps a member of his court (Antipas left Palestine in 39 CE and was banished to Gaul).

Matthias: Shortly following Jesus' ascension, Peter led the Jerusalem believers, about 120 strong, to select someone to replace Judas Iscariot as an apostle, for Judas had first betrayed Jesus by aiding in his arrest and then had committed suicide. In stating the need for someone to take Judas' place, Peter quoted Psalm 109:8, presenting it as a prophecy about Judas' untimely death and his office being assumed by another. The community of believers put forward two men as candidates. The criterion was that they had been followers of Jesus throughout His earthly ministry and were witnesses of His post-resurrection appearances and ascension. The two selected were Joseph Justus (Barsabbas) and Matthias. After praying, the congregation cast lots, and the lot fell to Matthias.

Mnason of Cyprus: Paul, on the return leg of his 3rd missionary journey—his last journey to Jerusalem, ca. 57 CE—came to Caesarea Maritima and met with the believers there. These disciples then accompanied Paul and his party (presumably including Luke, the narrator) on the way up to Jerusalem, perhaps to attend the major Jewish pilgrim feast of Pentecost, or Shavuot (Acts 20:16). On this journey, the Caesarea disciples "brought with them" (the KJV says) one Mnason of Cyprus with whom Paul was to lodge. Other translations make it clear that they *brought Paul to* Mnason. If Mnason in fact lived in Jerusalem, his home is probably the setting of the glad reunion of Acts 21:17. That Mnason was an "old" disciple (KJV) meaning an early disciple, one of long standing.

Nicanor: The need for special servants within the Jerusalem church was prompted by complaints of unfairness in distributing the community's resources, an inequity based on cultural distinctions (Acts 6:1). In the larger Jewish world, jealousy had long existed between (1) the "Hebrews," who spoke mostly Aramaic and read the scriptures in Hebrew and (2) "Grecians," Hellenized Jews who spoke Greek and read the Septuagint version of the Bible. Besides these cultural differences, it may be that the Hellenists also held a less strict interpretation of Torah. Regardless, it should not be surprising that such conflicts within Judaism would carry over into the primitive Judeo-Christian community. So as not to divert the apostles from their spiritual functions of prayer and preaching, the church set apart seven men "of honest report, full of the Holy Ghost and wisdom" to tend to everyday administrative matters (Acts 6:2-4). There seems to be a spiritual aspect to the office as well, for at least two of those appointed, Philip and Stephen, preached and did "the work of evangelists." In Acts 21:8 these special servants seem to have become known collectively as "the seven." It is worth noting that, from their names (Acts 6:5), all of the men chosen appear to belong to the Hellenist faction which had complained of being slighted. Also of interest is the democratic process at work in the church: the men are chosen by the whole community, then "ordained" by the apostles (Acts 6:6). Nothing more is known of Nicanor.

Nicolas: The need for special servants within the Jerusalem church was prompted by complaints of unfairness in distributing the community's resources, an inequity based on cultural distinctions (Acts 6:1). In the larger Jewish world, jealousy had long existed between (1) the "Hebrews," who spoke mostly Aramaic and read the scriptures in Hebrew and (2) "Grecians," Hellenized Jews who spoke Greek and read the Septuagint version of the Bible. Besides these cultural differences, it may be that the Hellenists also held a less strict interpretation of Torah. Regardless, it should not be surprising that such conflicts within Judaism would carry over into the primitive Judeo-Christian community. So as not to divert the apostles from their spiritual functions of prayer and preaching, the church set apart seven men "of honest report, full of the Holy Ghost and wisdom" to tend to everyday administrative matters (Acts 6:2-4). There seems to be a spiritual aspect to the office as well, for at least two of those appointed, Philip and Stephen, preached and did "the work of evangelists." In Acts 21:8 these special servants seem to have become known collectively as "the seven." It is worth noting that, from their names (Acts 6:5), all of the men chosen appear to belong to the Hellenist faction which had complained of being slighted. Also it is interesting to note the democratic process at work in the church: the men were chosen by the whole community, then "ordained" by the Apostles (Acts 6:6). Of Nicolas himself, we know only that he was a "proselyte of Antioch," i.e. a Gentile convert, either to Judaism first or perhaps directly into the Judeo-Christian community.

Parmenas: The need for special servants within the Jerusalem church was prompted by complaints of unfairness in distributing the community's resources, an inequity based on cultural distinctions (Acts 6:1). In the larger Jewish world, jealousy had long existed between (1) the "Hebrews," who spoke mostly Aramaic and read the scriptures in Hebrew and (2) "Grecians," Hellenized Jews who spoke Greek and read the Septuagint version of the Bible. Besides these cultural differences, it may be that the Hellenists also held a less strict interpretation of Torah. Regardless, it should not be surprising that such conflicts within Judaism would carry over into the primitive Judeo-Christian community. So as not to divert the apostles from their spiritual functions of prayer and preaching, the church set apart seven men "of honest report, full of the Holy Ghost and wisdom" to tend to everyday administrative matters (Acts 6:2-4). There seems to be a spiritual aspect to the office as well, for at least two of those appointed, Philip and Stephen, preached and did "the work of evangelists." In Acts 21:8 these special servants seem to have become known collectively as "the seven." It is worth noting that, from their names (Acts 6:5), all of the men chosen appear to belong to the Hellenist faction which had complained of being slighted. Also of interest is the democratic process at work in the church: the men are chosen by the whole community, then "ordained" by the apostles (Acts 6:6). Nothing more is known of Parmenas.

Peter (Simon Peter): Peter, one of the twelve disciples of Jesus, was one of the three closest to Christ during Hs earthly ministry, along with James and John, whom he had previously been fishing partners with (Luke 5: 7, 10). His brother Andrew, a former disciple of John the Baptist, first introduced him to Jesus (John 1:35-42). Jesus said of Peter:

Matthew 16:18 "...thou art Peter, and upon this rock I will build my church; and the gates of hell shall not prevail against it." (KJV).

Peter, though he failed many times, showed possibly a greater, more zealous love for Jesus than the other disciples. When Jesus walked on the Sea of Galilee, Peter was the only one who stepped out onto the water though he began to sink because of fear (Matthew 14:22-33). When Jesus asked the disciples who they thought He was, Peter answered and said,

"Thou art the Christ, the Son of the living God" (Matthew 16:16- KJV).

Even at the "Last Supper" it was Peter who first to declared that he would not deny Christ Jesus, though he later did three times (Matthew 26:31-35, 69-75). Jesus later restored him to the faith and Peter was a great leader in the church from that time on. Peter was one of the first to take the Good News to the Gentiles, to Cornelius the Roman centurion (Acts 10), though Peter mainly spread the Good News to the Jews, while Paul went to the Gentiles (Galatians 2:9). On the day of Pentecost, Peter explained to the confused, yet amazed crowd, from the Scriptures what was happening, explaining Who Jesus is, and how to be saved. On that day, about three thousand believed and were baptized (Acts 2). Later, Peter and John boldly spoke to the Sanhedrin in regards to their opposition of the Gospel, declaring the great power of God, and that salvation comes through Christ Jesus alone (Acts 4:1-22).

Philip the Evangelist: Philip the Evangelist (not to be confused with the apostle of the same name) first appears in Acts 6 where he is one of seven special servants chosen and ordained by the Church in Jerusalem. These men—all with Greek names—were to oversee the community's charitable distributions after the Greek-speaking believers complained about being slighted in favor of "the Hebrews." Among "the seven" (often regarded as "deacons," although that Greek word is not used), Stephen and Philip are mentioned as having special evangelistic ministries as well. In Acts 8:4ff, Philip goes to Samaria and preaches there with great success, his influence extending to Simon the Sorcerer, drawn to Philip's ministry by the "miracles and signs" which he performed. When Peter and John came, they imbued the Samaritan believers with the Holy Spirit, whereas Philip had only baptized them "in the name of the Lord Jesus." Philip then, prompted by an angel, travels south and on the Jerusalem-Gaza road encounters the treasurer of the Queen of Ethiopia (Acts 8:26ff). The man is returning to his homeland by chariot after worshipping in Jerusalem, reading the Hebrew Scriptures on the way. In response to Philip's message, the Ethiopian believes in Christ and is immediately baptized. That the Spirit of the Lord then "caught away Philip" - usually taken to mean he was supernaturally transported from that place; then, being "found at" Azotus (Ashdod), where he proceeded on to Caesarea (Acts 9:39-40). One final mention of Philip—now called "the evangelist"—has him residing with his family in Caesarea

Maritima, when Paul comes there on his final journey to Jerusalem ca. 57 CE (Acts 21:8).

Priscilla (Prisca): Priscilla and her husband Aquila—always mentioned together—were Jewish followers of Jesus in Corinth, where they offered Paul lodging in their home and became fellow-workers with him, both in the trade of tent-making and in spreading the gospel of Christ (Acts 18:1-3). The couple had settled in Corinth after being expelled from Rome, victims of the edict of Claudius against the Jews in 49/50 CE. That they were owners of property and able to travel widely suggests they had considerable financial means. Aquila and Priscilla, after encountering Paul in Corinth, traveled with him as far as Ephesus, where they lived and apparently hosted a house-church for the believers. There they also met the Christian preacher Apollos, whom they gently taught and corrected when they found his message lacking (Acts 18:26). Aquila and Priscilla apparently later returned to Rome (after the edict was lifted in 54 CE) and became prominent in the Christian community there as well (Rom. 16:3). As supporters of Paul—to the point of putting themselves in danger (Rom. 16:4)—and as leaders in the various churches, this couple's value to the apostle is reflected in the frequent greetings addressed to them in Paul's letters.

Prochorus: The need for special servants within the Jerusalem church was prompted by complaints of unfairness in distributing the community's resources, an inequity based on cultural distinctions (Acts 6:1). In the larger Jewish world, jealousy had long existed between (1) the "Hebrews," who spoke mostly Aramaic and read the scriptures in Hebrew and (2) "Grecians," Hellenized Jews who spoke Greek and read the Septuagint version of the Bible. Besides these cultural differences, it may be that the Hellenists also held a less strict interpretation of Torah. Regardless, it should not be surprising that such conflicts within Judaism would carry over into the primitive Judeo-Christian community. So as not to divert the apostles from their spiritual functions of prayer and preaching, the church set apart seven men "of honest report, full of the Holy Ghost and wisdom" to tend to everyday administrative matters (Acts 6:2-4). There seems to be a spiritual aspect to the office as well, for at least two of those appointed, Philip and Stephen, preached and did "the work of evangelists." In Acts 21:8 these special servants seem to have become known collectively as "the seven." It is worth noting that, from their names (Acts 6:5), all of the men chosen appear to belong to the Hellenist faction which had complained of being slighted. Also of interest is the democratic process at work in the church: the men are chosen by the whole community, then "ordained" by the apostles (Acts 6:6). Nothing more is known of Prochorus.

Rhoda: During a Passover season persecution of the primitive Jerusalem church by Herod Agrippa I (ruled Palestine 41-44 CE), Peter was imprisoned and his fellow believers prayed for him "without ceasing." The night before his public trial was to be held Peter was miraculously released through the intervention of an angel and proceeded to the house of Mary, mother of John Mark, where the believers were accustomed to gathering. When Peter knocked at the door, the young girl Rhoda responded, heard and recognized Peter's voice, and was so overcome with joy that she rushed back inside to announce his presence—but neglected to open the door for him! Those assembled at first dismissed the girl's report, suggesting she was mad or that it was "his angel." Only at his persistent knocking did they finally let Peter in, astonished at the reality of his deliverance (Acts 12:12-16).

Secundus the Macedonian: Known only from a passing reference in Acts 20:4, Secundus is one of at least seven men accompanying Paul on the return leg of his third missionary journey (ca. 55 CE), as they cross from Europe into Asia. Secundus is one of two men mentioned from the Macedonian city of Thessalonica, the other being Aristarchus. These companions may have been helping Paul gather money from the Gentile churches as a contribution to the poor in Jerusalem (2 Cor. 8:1—9:5). Also, if some were Jewish converts, they may have been bound for Jerusalem, to attend the great pilgrim festival of Pentecost (Shavuot) (Acts 20:16).

Silas: Silas is identified in Acts 15 as a leader and prophet in the Jerusalem church. He and Judas Barsabbas were sent along with Paul and Barnabas to take the apostolic decrees from the Jerusalem conference to the church at Antioch. This letter of instruction said that Gentile believers were not bound to fully observe the Mosaic Law and, specifically, that circumcision was not required for salvation (Acts 15:1-2, 23-29). Silas remained in Antioch, assisted Paul in his evangelistic labors there, and then, after Paul and Barnabas parted ways over the issue of John Mark, was chosen by Paul to be his companion on the second missionary tour (Acts 15:36-40). Two of Silas' credentials would have made him especially useful to Paul: his Roman citizenship (Acts 16:37-38) and, as a source of theological legitimacy, an early connection with the Jerusalem church (and possibly "apostle" status—see 1 Thess. 2:6). The journey took them through Asia Minor and Macedonia and as far as Greece. At Lystra, the young Timothy joined their ministry (Acts 16:1-2), and at Troas they received the "Macedonian call" (16:9). In Philippi they encountered Lydia, the "seller of purple" (16:12-16), delivered a young girl of a spirit (16-18), and were beaten and cast into prison where, after an earthquake, a Philippian jailer was converted (16:19-31). At Thessalonica their preaching caused a disturbance and they were forced to flee (17:1-9), but they were received more warmly in the next place, Berea (17:10-13). Silas and Timothy then remained for a time in Macedonia while Paul went on to Athens (17:14), but they later re-joined him at Corinth (Acts 18:5). Silas was active in the ministry there (2 Cor. 1:19) but is mentioned no more in the Acts narrative. Silas (as "Silvanus") is a co-author of Paul's Thessalonian epistles, the first of which was likely written *from* Corinth at this time, during the apostle's extended stay ca. 50 CE (Acts 18:11). So, it is possible Silas delivered this letter to the Thessalonian church and then remained in Macedonia, as he does not seem to be with Paul on the return leg of his journey (Acts 18:18). Later, "Silvanus" appears to be associated with Peter, as scribe or courier of that apostle's letter from Rome (1 Peter 5:12).

Simeon (Niger): Simeon Niger held a role as a special minister in the church of Antioch (Syrian Antioch, to distinguish from the one in Psidia in Asia Minor). He was among those who, first, served alongside Barnabas and Saul and then, at the prompting of the Holy Spirit, set them apart for a special work, ordained them with the laying on of hands, and sent them out (Acts 13:1). Simeon's Latin surname (Niger = "black") suggests that he was a dark-skinned African. [Some have supposed that this individual is the Simon of Cyrene who bore Christ's cross (Matt. 27:32), based on the similarity of the names, Cyrene's location on the N. coast of Africa, and the fact that some Cyrenian believers fled Jerusalem and went to Antioch (Acts 11:20).]

Simon the Tanner: Simon was a Christian believer, a tanner or leatherworker by trade, who lived in the coastal city of Joppa. When Peter was impelled to flee Jerusalem because of threats on his life, he came first to Lydda and then to Joppa, on his way to Caesarea. In Joppa he "tarried many days," lodging with Simon (Acts 9:28-30, 32, 41-43). While Peter was staying with Simon, two visions set the stage for the conversion of a Roman centurion stationed at Caesarea Maritima, the seat of Roman administration in Judea lying 30 mi./50 km up the coast from Joppa. The first vision is to Cornelius, instructing him to send men to Joppa, and bring Peter back to him (Acts 10:1-8). The second vision is to Peter, coming to him as he observed his mid-day prayers on Simon's rooftop. The prolonged vision, dealing with creatures considered unclean under Jewish ritual law, prepares Peter for crossing a formidable cultural barrier with the Gospel: setting aside the Jewish proscription against associating with Gentiles (Acts 10:9-16, 28). After the men from Caesarea came and took Peter to Cornelius, the centurion and his family believed, received the Holy Spirit, and were baptized—the Church's first recorded Gentile converts.

Sopater the Berean: Sopater is one of seven men identified as travelling with Paul through Macedonia and into Asia, on the return leg of the apostle's 3rd missionary journey and final trip to Jerusalem, ca. 55 CE. He may have been among the Jewish converts in Berea who previously "received the word with all readiness" (Acts 17:10-12). Nothing else is known of him for certain from the Scriptures, unless the "Sosipater" who sends his greetings in Rom. 16:21 is the same individual, which is likely. If so, and if Paul's reference in Romans to "my kinsmen" is taken to mean fellow-Jews, then in Acts 20 Sopater was probably accompanying Paul all the way to Jerusalem, sharing his desire to reach there in time for the great pilgrim festival of Pentecost (Heb., *Shavuot*, "weeks") (Acts 20:16).

Sosthenes: He was the synagogue ruler who was seized and beaten in Corinth (Acts 18:17), immediately after the Jews brought Paul before the Roman proconsul and tried unsuccessfully to have their complaints against him heard.

Gallio, the proconsul, considered the charges spurious—arcane matters of Jewish law—and had refused to hear the case (Acts 18:14-15). Although the KJV says "all the Greeks" attacked Sosthenes, the text simply reads "they," so the identity and motivation of the perpetrators are not readily apparent. Most likely, a group of Gentile onlookers (Greek or Roman), in the charged atmosphere of the Jews' forcible eviction from the tribunal (Acts 18:16), attack Sosthenes either from purely anti-Semitic impulses or to punish the Jews for troubling a high Roman official with seemingly trivial religious matters. [Some identify this Sosthenes with another person of the same name, the co-author with Paul of 1 Corinthians (1 Corinthians 1:1). If the two are indeed the same individual, Sosthenes became a believer and traveled to Ephesus where the epistle of 1 Corinthians was written (1 Cor. 16:8), perhaps as part of the delegation from Corinth mentioned in 1 Cor. 16:17-18.]

Theophilus: Theophilus was the person to whom both the Gospel of Luke and the Book of Acts were addressed, and nothing else is known of him for certain from the scriptures. The form of address, "most excellent"—the same title Paul uses in addressing Felix (Acts 23:26; 24:3) and Festus (Acts 26:25)—suggests a person of some rank, perhaps a Roman officer or high government official. Because Acts ends with Paul still in prison, some have suggested a corresponding early date for its writing, in the early 60s CE, and, given this scenario, some have guessed that Theophilus might be Paul's lawyer in Rome. Another possibility set forward is that the name is actually used as a literary device and does not represent a specific historical person. In this case, the "friends of God," the intended audience of Luke-Acts, could be the Church at large, generic seekers or inquirers into the Christian message, or perhaps specifically the Gentiles aligned with Judaism known as "God-fearers."

Timon: The need for special servants within the Jerusalem church was prompted by complaints of unfairness in distributing the community's resources, an inequity based on cultural distinctions (Acts 6:1). In the larger Jewish world, jealousy had long existed between (1) the "Hebrews," who spoke mostly Aramaic and read the scriptures in Hebrew and (2) "Grecians," Hellenized Jews who spoke Greek and read the Septuagint version of the Bible. Besides these cultural differences, it may be that the Hellenists also held a less strict interpretation of Torah. Regardless, it should not be surprising that such conflicts within Judaism would carry over into the primitive Judeo-Christian community. So as not to divert the apostles from their spiritual functions of prayer and preaching, the church set apart seven men "of honest report, full of the Holy Ghost and wisdom" to tend to everyday administrative matters (Acts 6:2-4). There seems to be a spiritual aspect to the office as well, for at least two of those appointed, Philip and Stephen, preached and did "the work of evangelists." In Acts 21:8 these special servants seem to have become known collectively as "the seven." It is worth noting that, from their names (Acts 6:5), all of the men chosen appear to belong to the Hellenist faction which had complained of being slighted. Also of interest is the democratic process at work in the church: the men are chosen by the whole community, then "ordained" by the apostles (Acts 6:6). Of Timon himself nothing more is specifically known.

Timothy: Timothy first appears in the Acts narrative as a young believer in Lystra whom Paul encounters early in his 2nd journey, ca.51-52 CE (Acts 16:1-3). Since Timothy here is already a "disciple" who is "well reported of" by the local believers, and since Paul had visited Lystra twice previously (Acts 14.8, 21) and later calls Timothy "my own son in the faith" (1 Tim.1:2), it is reasonable to suppose that Paul had been responsible for the young man's conversion. Now, choosing Timothy to travel and preach with him, Paul insisted on his circumcision (Acts 16:3). While Paul refused to burden *Gentile* believers with the Mosaic Law (cp. Gal. 2:3), Timothy, having a Jewish mother, *was* a Jew, albeit a seemingly assimilated and non-observant one. Paul knew that in Timothy's new role—frequently engaging other Jews over matters of religion—he would possess much greater legitimacy having been circumcised, especially since the people of the region "knew all that his father was a Greek." Timothy now accompanied Paul and Silas on the apostle's 2nd missionary journey, ca. 51-52 CE, through Asia Minor and into Macedonia (Acts 16:4-12), including the cities of Philippi, Thessalonica, and Berea (Acts 16-17). Timothy and Silas then remained in Macedonia, encouraging the churches there, while Paul went ahead to Athens (Acts 17:14; 1 Thess. 3:2). We next find him with Paul at Corinth, from where the Thessalonian letters were probably written (1 Thess. 1:1; 2 Thess. 1:1). Timothy later appears with Paul at Ephesus on the 3rd missionary journey, ca. 52-54 CE (Acts 19:22), and from there is sent on ahead on still another mission into Macedonia. Later in that same journey Timothy accompanied Paul from Macedonia back into Asia as he headed toward Jerusalem (Acts 20:4). When the apostle was a prisoner at Rome, Timothy joined him (Phil. 1:1) and was asked later in a letter to rejoin him and bring with him certain personal items left at Troas (2 Tim. 4:13). According to tradition, after Paul's death Timothy settled and ministered in Ephesus and died a martyr there.

Trophimus: Trophimus is a believer identified in Acts 20:4, (along with Tychicus) as being "of Asia" and accompanying Paul and others on the return leg of the apostle's 3rd missionary journey. In Acts 21:29 he is in Jerusalem and further identified as "an Ephesian" and presumably a Gentile. When some Jews see Paul in the Temple, in fulfillment of a vow, they mistakenly presume he had taken Trophimus—whom they had seen with Paul earlier—into the inner courts of the Temple, contrary to Jewish law. That these are Jews "of Asia" (i.e. Asia Minor) suggests they may have encountered Paul and his teachings (and Trophimus?) in their homeland and, like him, come to Jerusalem for Pentecost (Acts 20:16). Seizing Paul and beating him, these opponents incite a general disturbance in the Temple precincts, leading to Paul's arrest by Roman authorities. [A Trophimus is mentioned in 2 Tim 4:20 as being left behind by Paul at Miletus due to illness. If this is the same individual, it may imply that Paul was released from his Roman imprisonment, resumed activity in the East, and possibly imprisoned a second time.]

Tychicus: Tychicus was a believer identified in Acts 20:4, along with Trophimus, as being "of Asia" and accompanying Paul and others on the return leg of the apostle's 3rd missionary journey, from Macedonia to Jerusalem. From references to Tychicus in four different Pauline epistles (assuming it is the same individual), he appears to have served as Paul's co-worker and messenger, personally delivering his letters, including Ephesians and Colossians, during Paul's imprisonment in Rome. Tychicus is praised by Paul as a "beloved brother," a "faithful minister," and "fellow-servant in the Lord."

Paul's Response to the Roman World: The Book of Acts in the "New Testament" Collection

In addition to the writings OF Paul, we possess in the Bible writing ABOUT Paul that need our consideration. The historical context of Paul also has a literary context in the New Testament itself that is worth exploring...

The Bible term "New Testament" refers to a collection of twenty-seven first century writings that became the foundation of the faith and practice of Christianity. The collection was written primarily in the Greek language, the common language of the Roman world of that day. It contains four distinct types of literature: A biographical series on Jesus of Nazareth called the "Gospels;" an historical narrative of the progress of the early Messianic Jews and their later Gentile converts; personal letters called "Epistles;" and apocalyptic literature.

The four Gospels are named after their understood authors: Matthew, Mark, Luke and John. They chronicle selective accounts of the life and work of Jesus of Nazareth in first century Judea, Samaria and Galilee. The historical narrative of the early movement of the followers of Jesus the Messiah (called "Messianics" in Hebrew or "Christians" after "Christos") - the Greek translation of the Hebrew term "Messiah") is called the Book the Acts. Following the narrative are twenty-one letters of several early movement leaders, named either by the writer they are attributed to or by the city or person of their destination. The collection closes with one apocalyptic work (a prophetic literary form like Daniel of the Hebrew Bible).

The name "New Testament" was taken from the words of Jesus recorded in the Gospel According to Luke (cp. Luke 22:20). The term "testament" means a covenant or an agreement between God and man. In the case of the "new" covenant, the implication was that recent events had initiated a remarkable change in the relationship between God and man. The New Testament's theme, therefore, is that a new provision had been made in the series of agreements (covenants) that God had made for His relationship with men, the terms of which are announced in these writings.

The collected writings of the New Testament span a remarkable variety of accounts, places, cultural settings and characters. As indicated, the record begins with the four accounts of the life and work of Jesus of Nazareth - a religious Jew of the early first century. The narrative traces His lineage, His birth in Bethlehem, His early life and childhood in the Galilee, His baptism in the Jordan River and His public ministry throughout Judea, Samaria, Perea and the Galilee. Jesus never wrote a book, and none of the account is from His hand. The accounts of His life and teaching were authored by several early followers (called "disciples") of Jesus as well as some who never met Jesus personally (i.e. Luke the Physician). The four books act as early pamphlets to share the heart of the work and message of Jesus. The climax of each account is the cruel execution of Jesus by Roman crucifixion, and the victorious narrative of His Resurrection from the dead.

The disciples of Jesus took His teaching and the story of His Resurrection to many parts of the Roman world. They called on people to believe that Jesus was not only the long-awaited Messiah promised to the Jewish people in the Hebrew Bible, but also the very Son of God that came in human form for all mankind (cp. Acts 17:32; Philippians 2). They spread a message referred to as the "good news" or literally "gospel" (Gr. *euangellion*). The core of this message was that God was singular in essence but multiple in personality. Jesus was God's Son that came in the human flesh to the earth to fulfill a mission of bringing man into a relationship with the God of Abraham. The redemption price of mankind was the blood of Jesus, sacrificed like a lamb at Passover for the sins of men. They taught that God had accepted the death of Jesus as a sacrifice "once for all" (Heb. 10:11-14) and that all men, regardless of their race or background could be fully accepted by God if they trust the work of Jesus as the basis of their redemption. As emissaries of this message, they became known as "Apostles" (Gr. *apostello*, "one sent").

The fifth book of the New Testament collection (called "The Acts of the Apostles", or "Book of Acts") is in part a travel diary of the pioneers of the gospel, and part an explanation of the issues and problems of the early communities of faith. These communities were called churches or congregations. The major theme of the book is an explanation of how the promised Messiah to the Jews became a part of the lives of many who were born Gentile. As non-Jews, they did not appear to be included in the promise of the Messiah, and most had never considered their need to be brought into a relationship with the God of the Hebrews.

The Author - Luke the Physician

Early church fathers of the first several centuries gave extensive witness that the third gospel was written by the "beloved physician" Luke (cp. Col. 4:14), the companion of Saul of Tarsus (also called the Apostle Paul). If this is in fact the case, the writer of this gospel was the only non-Jewish author of any book of the New Testament. There is ample internal evidence that he was likely a proselyte to Judaism who came to believe Jesus was the Messiah. In addition, we could surmise that the work was influenced by the preaching and teaching of Paul, in addition to the accounts of eyewitnesses collected (Luke 1:2).

Many scholars believe that Luke was from Macedonia, perhaps a Philippian by birth. It is interesting to note that in the accounts of Paul's journeys the author apparently joins Paul just before his dream of the Macedonian man that changed the course of Paul's journey toward Macedonia (Acts 16:9ff). The dream corresponds with the author changing the pronouns of the journey from "they" to "we" suggesting that the author is now an eyewitness to that part of the journey. The same happens when Paul reached Troas on his third journey to the area (Acts 20:6). The final selection of "we" passages is the trip of Paul from Caesarea to Rome (Acts 27 and 28). It is likely these reflect that Luke was with Paul all the way to Rome and wrote the letter that became this "book" from that city.

A brief review of the Gospel According to Luke (Epic one)

The Gospel according to Luke appears as part of a series of personal letters to a man named Theophilus who was seeking information on the work of Jesus of Nazareth. The letter opens with a statement of the primary purpose of the account. By the time of the writing of this gospel, the writer claims that "many others had taken in hand to write the things which Jesus said and did" (cp. Luke 1:1-4) and this account therefore was a collection of eyewitness accounts that focused on the *chronology* of the life of Jesus.

The structure of the letter includes some unusual features. In addition to the special attention to medical matters (as one would expect from a medical doctor when authoring a work - 4:38; 8:55), it also includes the most complete view of the events surrounding the birth and early life of Jesus. As a collection of reports, Luke has a keen interest in revealing a personal side of the ministry of Jesus, and takes specific care in personal accounts of Jesus with people like Zacchaeus of Jericho (Luke19), and a thankful healed leper in Galilee (Luke 17). His account is as full and careful as any other, but he offers special detail to the questionings and trials of Jesus, and to the scene of the Crucifixion. His Resurrection narratives include a long story of the personal encounter of some followers of Jesus that discover the Risen One as they travel the road to Emmaus. His citations of the Hebrew Bible lead some scholars to wonder if Theophilus (the recipient of the letter) may have been a Greek speaking Jew, or at least a proselyte familiar with some Jewish discussions and Scriptures. This occurs also in the Acts sequel, where Luke tells the time of the year by the Jewish feasts (Acts 27:9).

The Theme of the Book of Acts (Epic two)

The style of the writing of the Gospel according to Luke and the subsequent opening of the Book of Acts both suggest that this was a series of letters written to share the progress of the Gospel from its inception to the work of the early congregations and Messianic leaders. Perhaps along with the Gospel of Luke and the Book of Acts, there was a third document intended but never completed or lost in history (an unfinished trilogy?). Some speculate on a third letter, an idea fueled by the incomplete ending in the Book of Acts. Luke was an otherwise thorough author. The main characters and several issues are left unresolved, as though more were to follow.

The journey to Rome is given in an eyewitness account, and may indicate one underlying purpose of Luke's letter. It may have been written to express to Theophilus "I guess you are wondering how a physician from Philippi ended up in Rome attending a Jewish prisoner. Well it all started a long time ago when..."

Another theme is woven into the end of the account in Paul's words from his final recorded sermon. In Rome the Jews refused to hear of God's fulfillment of the Messianic promise in Jesus of Nazareth, so he took the message to the Gentiles. It seems important for Luke to point out to Theophilus that the Gospel was taken to the Jew first, but then presented to the Gentile as a result of continual resistance on the part of some in various synagogues. Paul consistently offered the Gospel "to the Jew first" as Paul reminds the Romans in his Epistle to them (Romans 1:16). When refused more opportunity by resistance, he turned "also to the Greek." This seems to be highlighted in the accounts of Paul's major works in each mission journey: at Pisidian Antioch (Acts 13:46) in the First Mission Journey; at Corinth (18:6) in the Second Mission Journey; and at Ephesus (19:9) in the Third Mission Journey. If part of the intent was not a treatise in defense of Paul's methodology, Luke seems to be preoccupied with it.

It is also worth noting that Luke seems intent on showing that the Messianic movement and its counterpart in the Gentile world is not a subversive movement. On no less than nine separate records (Acts 13:7ff; 16:19-39; 17:6-9; 17:18-34; 18:12-17; 19:31ff; 24:23-27; 25:14-21; 26:30-32), Luke carefully records the defense of Christian thought and practice as harmless to the Roman political system. It appears this was a concern by rulers like Felix, Festus and several local magistrates.

Finally, any student can readily recognize in implication in the opening words to Theophilus that Luke intended the previous record (i.e. the Gospel According to Luke)to unfold that which Jesus "began to do and teach" (Acts 1:1). A stated purpose of the narrative was to unfold that which Jesus continued to teach, through His Holy Spirit and His Church. One understanding may be that Luke envisioned the Hebrew Scriptures as capturing the work of the Father in Heaven, while the Gospel revealed the work of the Son. In this work, he desired to highlight the work of the Holy Spirit in unity with the other texts.

Paul's Response to the Roman World:
The Story of the Book of Acts

This second letter written to Theophilus continues the story of the spread of the Gospel that he began in the <u>Gospel According to St. Luke</u>. This second epic opens with Jesus (after His death and resurrection) meeting His disciples and instructing them in Jerusalem. Jesus told them to gather and wait there until the coming of the Holy Spirit and then He ascended into Heaven. His disciples went back to Jerusalem and selected a replacement for Judas by casting lots. They narrowed the choices by character to two men: Joses (called Barnabas) and Matthias, who was eventually chosen. [Chapter 1]

A short time later on the day of Pentecost, the disciples were together in Jerusalem praying and the Holy Spirit came upon them. This enabled them to tell the good news about the Lord in many languages that they had never learned before an international crowd of Jews gathered for the Feast. Peter followed the initial incident with an address to the excited and perplexed crowd explaining from the prophet Joel and from the words of David what had begun that day in their presence. He proclaimed salvation through faith in Messiah and more than three thousand people were saved. [Chapter 2]

These new "Messianics" were becoming known in Jerusalem, and began to care for one another. One afternoon at the gate of the Temple, Peter and John healed a crippled beggar who was asking for help. This caused quite a stir, as the people recognized him from the many times they passed by him and now saw that he could walk. They gathered around Peter and he explained that the power that healed the man was the power of the risen Messiah! He told the people they were guilty of killing Jesus, but that they could be forgiven of their sins by repenting and turning to the Lord. Peter and John were swiftly arrested and brought before the Jewish religious authorities who questioned them about the healing. They could find no wrongdoing by Peter and John and could not deny the healing of the crippled man, but they wished them to cease causing a stir among the people. They threatened the two and sent them on their way, recognizing the numbers of Messianic followers of Jesus were swelling to about five thousand! [Chapters 3-4]

The Messianic believers still worshipped in the courts of the Temple (mostly associated with Solomon's Porch on the east side of the Temple plaza) and shared what they had with each other. Some sold property and then gave the proceeds to the apostles to distribute it as there was a need. These heartfelt acts of giving became marks of the followers of Jesus, and others began to mimic the giving, though not always for honest reasons, or with an honest heart. One such couple, Ananias and Sapphira sold a piece of land but kept some of the money back for themselves. When presenting the money to the disciples they evidently lied about the amount they were giving, making a show of the gift. Ananias died on the spot before the apostles. When his wife came shortly after, she also lied about the amount of money and fell over dead and was buried alongside her husband. News of the event made all of the believers carefully consider their hearts, and began a long journey of the need to constantly renew their walk with God. This internal situation was but the first challenge or test to the fledgling movement.

Because the group continued to gain in strength, the Temple leadership decided they needed to take action and imprison some of the Messianic leaders. While awaiting the hearing, an angel opened the cell and told the Messianic leaders to go back and preach in the Temple courts, so they left the cell and returned to the work. The High Priest was informed about the "escape" and had them brought into the council chamber for an immediate hearing. The Messianic leaders explained their message, and refused to refrain from preaching it. Fearing the response of the crowds and listening to some of the more moderate voices in the chamber, the Temple leadership allowed them to leave, and they continued to spread the message daily. [Chapter 5]

As the size of the work grew, the needs of those who joined to the message grew. The leadership was taxed, as it was not able to both seek the face of the risen Savior and care for all the followers in a way that met their needs. A third test faced the Messianics as some were complaining about the uneven meeting of needs. It appeared to the Diaspora (Greek speaking) followers of Jesus that they were getting neglected in comparison to the local Hebrew speaking followers. New leaders of character and faith were chosen, and the problem was handled by better organization.

During the time the Messianics were increasing in numbers, their message was being discussed all over Jerusalem, and the theological schools no doubt became heated with discussions of the merits of their claims. Some students decided to directly attack the Messianics, wholly disagreeing with the basic tenets of their message. Of the new group of seven Messianic servant leaders, one man named Stephen was singled out by a local Jewish Seminary for Diaspora students as a target of their wrath. After a lengthy defense which Stephen put before them and which they could not answer, they called on the Temple leadership to rescue them from the debate, and Stephen was brought before the council at the Temple. A long sermon followed, which illustrated the value of carefully examining the choice of these new servant leaders, and Stephen offered his defense of the Messianic message. He called on them to remember their history and the promises of God, and then told them Messiah had already come. Angry at his words, they took him beyond the wall of Jerusalem and stoned him there. One student held the coats, and stared as Stephen's blood was spilt. He was Saul of Tarsus, who later became an important figure in the Messianic community. [Chapters 6-7]

Saul took on the attack of Messianics with great zeal, entering houses of suspected followers of Jesus and bringing them to prison. The followers began to separate and spread out, with some of the Diaspora Jews heading to their home countries with their new message. That was not the only way the good news that Messiah had come spread, however. God directed some like Philip, who was one of the servant leaders chosen by the people at the same time Stephen was chosen, to take the message to places in Samaria. After some remarkable movements of the Spirit of God there, Philip was compelled to go south along the road to Gaza. While moving along the road, he came upon a noble eunuch reading about the promise of Messiah, and Philip had the opportunity to share with him that Messiah's promise had been fulfilled in Jerusalem. The eunuch had a desire to walk with the God of Abraham, but was not allowed to enter the Temple as a deformed man. After the man received his first opportunity of baptism, and knew God really accepted him, Philip sensed his mission there was complete, and left for Caesarea, preaching as he traveled. [Chapter 8]

Saul of Tarsus continued to cause real trouble for the Messianics; he had official letters allowing him to extend his search for Messianics to Damascus, trying to contain the spread of this growing Jewish movement. While on his way there, he was struck down on the road, and heard the voice of this same Jesus that the Messianics were talking about. He left the experience blind, with a promise that God was about to tell him what he should do for Him. Led by the hand, his companions brought him into Damascus, and Saul fasted three days waiting for instructions from God. Finally they came, and he was directed to Ananias, a man who had been given directions from God to lead Saul in his first steps of Messianic faith. Sight restored, Saul stayed for a time to share time with a small group of believers in Jesus. In a short time Saul began to preach the Messianic message in local synagogues, angering crowds that thought he was coming to shut down the Messianics. Some planned to kill Saul to stop the "defection" to the new message, and Saul escaped back to Jerusalem, being let down over the wall of Damascus in a basket. He was led by Barnabas (the one who was not chosen to join the twelve in the cast lots at the beginning of the story), and taken to meet the Messianic leadership. He remained a short time in Jerusalem, debating some from his old seminary, and eventually returned home to Tarsus.

While Saul created a stir in the movement, yet another small group of followers faced intense pain over the loss of one of their key members. Shimon, called Peter, one of the disciples of Jesus who now helped lead the Messianic movement, was making his way southwest of Jerusalem, and had opportunity to heal some who were sick. The small group at Joppa heard of the healings and called on Peter to care for their loss, and return their dear one named Tabitha to life and health. Peter came and prayed for Tabitha, and her body was restored, causing the whole group to rejoice! Peter went to the house of another Shimon, who was a tanner, to remain with this small group for a time.

One afternoon, hungry and awaiting a meal, Peter was on the roof of Shimon's house, and had a vision sent from God. The vision was of a sheet filled with animals that God had forbidden his people to eat. A voice told Peter to kill the animals and eat, but three times he refused, standing firm on God's command. In the midst of the vision, a knock on the door of Shimon's house brought Peter back to the moment. A centurion named Cornelius sent three of his soldiers to call for Peter to come to him in Caesarea. Peter, realizing that the vision of the animals was to call him to follow these three men to the home of a Gentile, agreed to go with them on the following day to Cornelius. Peter offered the men lodging, and left the next morning. [Chapter 9]

After an eight-hour walk to Caesarea, Peter entered the house of the centurion and conversed with him, sharing with him and his household the good news of Messiah. God moved in the man's heart, and the Spirit of God caused Cornelius to speak in a language he had not learned. With such an amazing demonstration of the power of God on his life, even the Jews were amazed that the good news was breaking into the heart of a proselyte who was not even circumcised! Seeing the work of the Spirit, Peter commanded Cornelius and his household to be baptized, and accepted them into the community of followers of Jesus. [Chapter 10]

News spread that Cornelius' house had joined the ranks of the believers, and soon the Jerusalem leadership found themselves in a debate about this new ministry direction. Men of the leadership called on Peter to account how he could "eat" with a Gentile. Peter recounted in detail the whole move of God in his life. The room fell silent, as men of God saw for the first time the direction toward which God was leading them. Peter finished, and the men agreed that God was opening the message to the Gentiles. They began to glorify God!

No sooner had the Jerusalem leadership acknowledged what God was beginning to do, than the Antioch believers began to see the door open in the hearts of Gentiles. Returning home when the persecutions, with arrests and Stephen's execution were going on in Jerusalem, a small fellowship of Messianics was established in Antioch, preaching Messiah had come to the

Jews. When they heard Gentiles were joining the movement, they opened the preaching of Messiah, and Gentiles responded. The Jerusalem Messianic leaders dispatched Barnabas to check out the growth. Thrilled with the work but seeing the need for depth in teaching, Barnabas went to Tarsus and brought back Saul to open a one-year series co-teaching the believers in Jesus at Antioch. During that year, a prophet had revealed that a famine was coming on the Roman world. The fellowships of Messianic followers and their new found Gentile believers took up a collection, and sent it to the Messianic leaders at Jerusalem to distribute it as they saw needs arise. The messengers entrusted to take the offering money to Jerusalem were Barnabas and Saul. [Chapter 11]

About the time the collection money was on its way, a government lead persecution of Messianics in Judea began under Herod Agrippa I. Herod decided the stir caused by the Messianic sect of Jews was an unhealthy influence on stability, and had James the son of Zebedee (brother of John), one of the Jesus' disciples executed. When he saw his favor grow in the Temple leadership as a result of the execution, he decided to further it by taking Peter into custody. Because of the Passover, Herod held Peter in prison for execution after the feast. While there, Peter was held between two soldiers, chained in a cell as the fellowship at Jerusalem prayed fervently for his release. Late one night, the angel of the Lord freed him and told him to dress himself, opening each gate and leading him out of the civil prison, as he had years before from the Temple guard. Peter came to the door of the small fellowship that was deep in prayer for him. Startling the local believers, he came to the share the news of release. He told them to tell the other leaders, and then left to stay in Caesarea. A short time later, Herod Agrippa died in Caesarea and the immediate threat abated. To add to that good news, the offering money arrived in Jerusalem. After a brief visit, Barnabas and Saul returned to Antioch with Barnabas' nephew, John Mark. [Chapter 12]

In Antioch, the worship time drew people into the presence of God. The Messianics began to be known as "Christians" (after the Greek term for Messiah). The Spirit instructed the believers to send out Barnabas and Saul to a work that He called them to. The congregation gathered together and sent them out with prayer and fasting. Departing Antioch with John Mark attending their needs, they walked to the port of Seleucia and caught a ship to Cyprus. Landing in Salamis, they preached the Messianic message in the synagogues and then traveled to Paphos on foot. While at Paphos, Saul and Barnabas were sent for by Sergius Paulus, the Proconsul. As they shared with the Proconsul their message, a certain sorcerer tried to keep him from believing. Saul (usually called "Paul" in Gentile areas) called on God to blind the sorcerer and he was blinded. Seeing this power, Sergius Paulus believed the message of Jesus.

Setting sail from Paphos, the three messengers of Messiah made their way north to Perga in Pamphylia. When they arrived in Perga, Paul was dominating the party. John Mark decided to depart the team and return to Jerusalem, apparently not liking the change in leadership. Paul (Saul) and Barnabas made their way through the Taurus mountain pass, and came into Antioch in Pisidia. That Sabbath, Paul preached a stirring message to the congregation about the coming of Messiah. Some Jews and some proselytes came to faith, while Gentiles requested that next week they be allowed to hear about Jesus. The following Sabbath Paul again preached to a vast group in the city, many of them Gentiles. Jews that had not believed the message of Jesus began to heckle them, but Barnabas and Paul spoke zealously that the message was to be for Gentiles as well, and many believed. The synagogue leaders who were against this preaching went to the city council and had the Messianics expelled. Paul and Barnabas moved on the nearby Iconium, but the believers in Pisidian Antioch remained and rejoiced in their newfound faith. [Chapter 13]

In Iconium, the Messianic messengers preached and debated, as many believed, both Jews and proselytes. After preaching and some amazing demonstrations of the power of God, the city was divided between those who believed and those who thought the message a hoax. Those who did not believe the message wanted to catch the men and stone them. Aware of the rising tide of trouble, Barnabas and Paul fled to the nearby Roman colony of Lystra in Lycaonia, a pagan city with no synagogue. Believing that God had opened the door for Gentiles to receive Messiah, they preached the good news that a relationship with the God of Abraham was possible for them. After healing a local boy who was born lame, people in the town began to worship them as manifestations of the pagan deities. As they assembled to offer sacrifices, Barnabas and Paul tore their clothes and begged the people to see them as mere men. After some time, some instigators of trouble came from Iconium and Pisidian Antioch and convinced the people of Lystra to have Paul stoned and left for dead. After the stoning, the believers gather outside the city around the body of Paul, and Paul got up and went home with them. The next day the men left Lystra and journeyed to Derbe, preaching to the people there. After a good response, they returned the way they came, checking on each small congregation as they returned through Lystra, Iconium and Pisidian Antioch. They returned to the coast of Pamphylia, preaching again in Perga, and returning to a ship at Attalia. They sailed back to Antioch filled with awe at what God had accomplished, and shared it for a season with the Antioch followers of Jesus. [Chapter 14]

In Antioch there were Messianic followers of Jesus from Judea who insisted, "One who is not circumcised according to the Torah of Moses cannot be justified before God." When Paul and Barnabas came to Antioch, they disagreed and a debate ensued. The question was submitted to Jerusalem's Messianic leadership, and a council of key figures of the movement was convened at Jerusalem. The debate was long and difficult. Peter argued that God had also chosen Gentiles and demonstrated that fact a long time ago. He saw no difference in the essential faith that lead to their justification, though in practice they remained different. He did not want the yoke of "living as a Jew" to be placed on their lives, with all its weight. Paul and Barnabas testified next, arguing that the work of the Spirit was clear in the lives of the Gentiles.

An Apostle named James (the half-brother of Jesus and writer of the Epistle of James) presided over the meeting, and brought the concluding judgment in the matter. He stated that God was at work in the Gentiles, and they had no place disregarding this fact. He disregarded the suggestion that Gentiles needed to physically identify with Israel's covenant symbol of circumcision and become part of Israel physically. He also distinguished the need for Gentiles to follow four specific commands that clearly separated them from their pagan past. He commanded that they: 1) abstain from idol offerings at pagan temples; 2) abstain from any pagan blood rituals; 3) abstain from idolatrous sacrifices even if they are bloodless and include only strangulation; 4) abstain from the sexual sin so much a part of their temple practices. In general, James said they must leave the paganism that pervaded their lives before, to clearly follow after Jesus. If they avoided these things and trusted in the atonement of Messiah alone for justification, they did not need to become a physical part of the Abrahamic covenant of promise to the sons of Isaac through Jacob, nor subject themselves to all the Torah standards associated with Israel's inheritance.

In addition to the pronouncement to the Gentiles, James made no change in the ruling concerning Torah commands to Jews, simply adding that Moses was explained to all of them in their home synagogues every Sabbath. With that, the council wrote the judgment in letters, and sent it out to the various congregations, restating the words of James. Letters were given to Paul and Barnabas to carry abroad to the congregations, while verbal testimony of Judas and Silas would reinforce the veracity of the report of the ruling. The letter was issued, and the teams were sent out to settle the matter in the congregations, beginning with Antioch.

Judas and Silas taught the ruling of the council to the congregation at Antioch, and Paul and Barnabas brought the letter. A short time passed and Paul asked Barnabas to accompany him on another outreach journey. The two could not agree on whether to offer another opportunity of participation to John Mark. Paul decided to go with Silas to the works in Pamphylia and Pisidia (the mainland areas of the previous journey), and Barnabas took John Mark to check on the Cypriot congregations (the island area of the previous journey). [Chapter 15]

Paul and Silas made their way through Syria past the famous battle site of Issus, and through the "Cilician gates" into Pisidia, where they visited the believers at Derbe and Lystra. At Lystra they added to their team a young man named Timothy of mixed birth (father Greek, mother Jewish), and Paul circumcised him. Paul knew the Jews of Pisidia would watch carefully how he treated the Torah in the life of a non-observant Jew. They saw the churches were growing and strong, and moved north and west through the lake district that lead to Phrygia, and into southern Galatia trying to move west to Asia Minor. The Spirit led them north to Mysia and the city of Troas near the Hellespont. When the team arrived in Troas, they met Luke the Physician, who had come from Macedonia (possibly from his home in Philippi). Paul was wrestling with the direction, and his desire to go into Asia Minor to great cities like Ephesus, Pergamon, Miletus and Smyrna. As he slept in Troas, a vision of a man from Macedonia (probably the physician Luke) called to him and requested help. Paul knew it was God's call to move west into Macedonia, so he immediately looked for a ship to take him across the northern Aegean Sea.

The four men took the boat from the harbor near Troas, and went overnight by ship to harbor in at Samothrace Island. The next day they moved on to Neapolis, where the team disembarked and traveled on foot over the mountain ridge to the Roman garrison and colony at Philippi. Finding no synagogue that Sabbath, the team made their way to the nearby stream to pray and worship (a common Jewish practice in such circumstances). At the stream, a Thyatiran woman named Lydia heard Paul speaking, and was drawn to the message of Messiah. Yielding her heart, she was baptized. Afterward, she asked the team to come to her home and stay there.

As they continued in the city, they had regular times of prayer and met together. During one such occasion a young demon-possessed slave girl kept harassing Paul and the others, and Paul commanded the demon to come out. With the exorcism, the owners of the slave girl lost the revenue her "gifts" provided, and complained to the magistrates of the city, falsely accusing Paul and Silas of subverting some Roman laws. The crowd seized the two, pulled off their clothes, beat them with lashes, and then imprisoned them without proper trial. Night fell, and Paul and Silas sat in their cell singing and praising God, when an earthquake opened the gates. The jailer saw the openings and thought he would be executed in humiliation when the prisoners under his charge escaped, but Paul cried out to him, "Do yourself no harm, we are all still here!" The jailer's heart melted and Paul and Silas shared the good news of Messiah with him. He accepted the message of Jesus, and took the men out of their cells to his home. He washed their wounds, and returned to the jail with them. In the morning the magistrates sent a message to let them go, but Paul refused to leave without an apology. Paul was a Roman citizen and was imprisoned and beaten without proper trial. When the magistrates heard he was Roman they came to him and asked him to leave town. Paul and Silas left the prison, visited Lydia and the other followers of Jesus, and then depart westward along the Via Egnatia. [Chapter 16]

Passing through the cities Amphipolis and Apollonia - Paul, Silas and Timothy headed directly to Thessalonica, where there was a Jewish community and a synagogue. Their host in the city was a man named Jason (and was likely a relative of Paul). The team arrived and Paul debated for three Sabbaths in the synagogue, explaining in detail that Messiah was promised and had come, suffering for them. A number of proselyte Greeks believed, as well as some prominent women in the synagogue. Among those who did not believe were some influential Jews who pressed a mob into pulling Jason from his house and placing him under bond. Paul agreed before the city council to leave and Jason was released. Paul and Silas said goodbye to the believers and slipped away in the night to Berea.

At Berea the team found an anxious audience that listened intently and tested everything that the Messianic teachers told them. Men and women both studied with them, and many believed, including some prominent proselyte men and women. Soon some of the Jews of Thessalonica who did not agree with the Messianic message found out about Paul and Silas' work in Berea, and came to disrupt the teaching. Those who believed gathered and determined it was best if Paul leave. Silas and Timothy remained in Macedonia, and Paul left to Athens alone by ship.

Paul's stay in Athens was a time of challenge. He was without the team, had experienced the pain of persecution, endured physical beating, and had an intense desire to go back to Thessalonica. Wrestling with these issues, he encountered the world center of pagan philosophy at Athens and was deeply stirred. He directed his first speaking in the synagogue but made no real progress. He turned his attention to the marketplace, encountering a number of philosophers and temple attendants. His preaching drew enough of a crowd that he was whisked off to the guardians of the teachings of the market, "the Areopagites." Paul offered a sermon that included quotes from two famous Greek poets and was mocked by some of the hearers. By the end of his time in Athens, he saw God draw a few to the faith, including Dionysos the Areopagite and a woman named Damaris, with a handful of others. Paul left alone on foot by way of the ceremonial Roman road that passed the Eleusian temple of Demeter and Persephony, and made his way to Corinth. [Chapter 17]

By the time Paul got to Corinth, discouragement set in and he needed a lift from God. The encouragement began in the form of some new Jewish friends named Aquila and Priscilla who shared the same craft of tent-making. Though he spoke each week in the synagogue, his real boldness to share the Messianic message returned when Silas and Timothy came and refreshed him with news from Macedonia. With poor reception from the officials in the synagogue (with the exception of the chief ruler named Crispus) Paul decided to turn his attention to reaching Gentiles in the city with his message. Many Corinthians believed and were baptized. Still Paul held back. He had suffered deep wounds on the journey, and needed a profound meeting with God. A vision came in the darkness of the night. Jesus came to Paul and assured him that if he would remain in the city, he would be protected from further attack. Paul believed, and remained there another eighteen months. It was apparent his promise to remain there became a vow before the Lord, not completed until the eighteen months was passed.

Even when tested before Gallio (the consul of Achaia), Paul knew that God would protect him. The new ruler of the synagogue (named Sosthenes) who replaced the now Messianic Crispus brought Paul to the judgment seat, but Gallio threw the case out. Then Sosthenes was taken and beaten by some locals with the court refusing to intervene. The disinterest of Gallio in perceived internal Jewish issues allowed the work to continue until the consul's term was over. Paul left about that time to the nearby eastern port of Cenchrea.

Looking out over the Saronic Gulf, Paul could see in his mind's eye all the way back to Jerusalem. It had been a long time since he was comfortably in the halls of the kosher friends at Jerusalem, and he missed them. He shaved his head, having completed his vow to serve Jesus in Corinth and gathered his friends for a farewell. He took a boat east with Aquila and Priscilla to Ephesus and spent a short time in the synagogue teaching. He left his friends there, and continued on to Caesarea, to the feast in Jerusalem, and eventually back to Antioch.

After some time, Paul decided to travel to the established congregations in Galatia and Phrygia. At the same time, other followers of Jesus were spreading the message to the Roman world. One such man was Apollos of Alexandria who was teaching and evangelizing effectively in Ephesus. He met Aquila and Priscilla there, and they added some details on baptism to his message that greatly aided him. After some challenging ministry in Ephesus, Apollos went on to Achaia and took up teaching believers in Jesus in Corinth. [Chapter 18]

While Paul was passing through Mysia venturing south to Ephesus, he came upon a group of a dozen believers that had been taught by Apollos before he was instructed in the work of the Spirit by Priscilla and Aquila. Paul told them of this work and they experienced powerful manifestations of it, prophesying and speaking in unlearned languages. Paul remained there, teaching in the synagogue for about three months, until he realized that no one else there would believe in Jesus. They took the believers next door to a local school, continuing to teach for two more years. God used Paul mightily, showing miraculous works through him, healings and the casting out of demons. Many idolaters turned to faith, and those in the black arts destroyed their evil books of incantations and spells.

After these years, Paul knew it was time to move on and check on the believers in Macedonia and Achaia. Paul saw things turning for the worse in Ephesus and delayed his departure for a bit. He sent Timothy and Erastus to check on the Macedonian believers. While they were gone, the Messianic believers got into trouble with the local guild of metal workers, who made their income by creating small replicas of pagan gods. Demetrius, the silversmith, led the riot to get rid of Paul, whose ministry was killing their market. Gaius and Aristarchius (both of Macedonia) were fellow workers of Paul. These two were caught and taken into the theatre. The town clerk saw the mob and tried to listen to their grievances, but finally dismissed the assembly as illegal. [Chapter 19]

Hostilities quieted and Paul felt he could leave. He journeyed to Mysia and came to Troas on foot. There he met a delegation of several friends that went before him into Macedonia and returned. This select group of friends included Sopater of Berea, Aristarchus and Secundus of Thessalonica, Luke the physician (probably of Philippi), Timothy of Lystra, and Tychicus and Trophimus of Ephesus. The whole group came to Troas after Passover, waiting there for Paul to join them. When Paul arrived they celebrated and shared in a meal together, followed by an extended study that lasted until dawn! During the meeting a young man named Eutychus fell asleep listening and tumbled from his spot on a window ledge to the floor. People gathered around and presumed him dead, but Paul came over him and raised him up. The people were relieved, but Paul got up and continued with the lesson! Paul sent the team by ship from Troas to Assos, but decided to walk alone and met them in there.

From Assos, Paul joined the team and sailed to Mytilene on Lesbos Island, harboring overnight. The next day they continued to Chios Island, another day to Samos Island (with an overnight at Trogyllium), and finally landed at Miletus. Paul had only been gone a short time out of Ephesus, but he felt that he may not get the chance to return to them in Asia Minor so he gathered the elders of the congregations together (including those of Ephesus). At Miletus, Paul delivered one of his most difficult emotional sermons. He told them they would not see him again, and they wept. After a time of prayer together, they took him to the ship and waved goodbye to this one who had shared the good news so tirelessly among them. [Chapter 20]

The ship journey took the team for brief stops at Cos, Rhodes and Patara. In Patara the team found a ship that was set to sail for the Phoenician coast. The ship sailed south of Cyprus directly to Tyre and offloaded her cargo. The team sought out local believers and met with them for seven days. During that time, several Messianic followers declared that the Spirit was warning Paul not to go up to Jerusalem. After the week of sharing, the believers prayed together and the team boarded a ship to head south. Following the coastline, they harbored the next day in Ptolemais, with time to visit the local believers there for one day. From Ptolemais, the team came into the great harbor at Caesarea.

At the modern and bustling port the team found their way to the house of Philip, one of the seven servant leaders chosen in Jerusalem years ago. Paul was in no hurry; he was refreshed to be back on Judean soil with a great company of friends from all over his ministry! While he was there, God sent a messenger to him, a prophet named Agabus (who had predicted the Roman world's famine years before). When the prophet came, he tied up Paul, and told the team that Paul was about to face such an arrest by Jews who did not agree that Messiah had come, and an imprisonment at the hands of the Gentiles. Though greatly urged to stay away from Jerusalem, Paul would not back off his plan and told them he was ready for what God had told them.

Hiring horses for the trip, Paul and the team made their way up to Jerusalem. Joining the ever-swelling ranks of the team were some Messianic followers from the Caesarea congregation, as well as Mnason of Cyprus, who had a house in Jerusalem. When they arrived in Jerusalem, the Messianic leaders warmly embraced the team, and assembled a meeting with James and all the leadership. They listened intently as Paul shared what God had done in the ministry to the Gentiles. They were excited to hear his account, but were also burdened by outside reports that had come back to them of his ministry.

Some had reported that Paul was telling Jews that lived in the Diaspora not to keep the Torah, but rather to forsake the ways of the inheritance that the Fathers had instructed them. The leadership reiterated the official finding of the Jerusalem Council, and made sure the team understood that their ruling was only for the Gentiles, and should not have affected the way the Jewish believers in Jesus behaved. They wanted to be clear, Gentiles needed to leave idolatry and cling to Jesus, but Jews needed to remain as Jews, clinging to justification through the blood of Messiah alone. To make the message clear that Paul was still walking according to the Torah, they instructed Paul to take four Jewish men who had taken a vow to the Jerusalem Temple to offer sacrifices. Paul did as he was instructed, was ritually bathed and got himself ready for seven days to bring the sacrifice necessary to complete the vow.

The day came to take the men, and Paul went into the Temple with the men as well as some of the Messianic team from Asia Minor. Some people in the Temple saw him and stirred up the people, accusing Paul of bringing in Gentiles to the inner court of the Temple, because they had seen him earlier in town with Trophimus, his team member from Ephesus. Paul was taken away and the inner court Temple doors were closed. The crowd gathered to kill him, pulling him toward the outer gate and beating him. Meanwhile, news came to the Roman guards of the adjacent Antonia Fortress that a riot had broken out. Roman soldiers were dispatched and took Paul from the hands of the angry crowd.

As he entered the fortress, Paul turned to the captain of the guard and spoke Greek to him. Startled, the captain asked his identity, and Paul identified himself as a Jew of Tarsus. He asked if he could address the people under the protection of the Roman guard on the stairway, and the captain agreed. Paul turned and spoke in Hebrew to the crowd. He delivered a powerful testimony to what God had done first in his life, then in the Messianic movement. When he reached the part of the message where God had sent him to Gentiles, the crowd roared and shook the dust of their sandals into the air. The captain ordered Paul brought inside. Binding him for a lashing, Paul told the soldiers he was a Roman citizen, and they warned their captain to be careful how they handled him. The captain came to him and asked him directly if he was a free citizen. When Paul made it clear that he was, the captain loosed him and kept him inside the Antonia. [Chapters 21-22]

The next day, Claudias Lysias (the captain of the guard) sent word that he wanted a meeting with the council and with Paul to settle the matter. Paul came before the council and proclaimed he was innocent of all charges. The High Priest commanded those who held him to strike him on the mouth. Paul chided the

High Priest (not knowing it was the High Priest) and complained that he was struck unlawfully. When the chamber called on Paul to reckon why he upbraided the High Priest, Paul apologized and told them he did not know whom it was that he was addressing (recognizing it was unlawful to chide the High Priest). When Paul saw the room was composed of both Pharisees (who believed in afterlife) and Sadducees (who did not), he proclaimed that he was a second generation Pharisee and was brought in because of his defense of resurrection and afterlife. The debate that ensued became a pulling match, and Claudius Lysias had Paul taken away, fearing he would be ripped apart in the scuffle. Paul was taken back to the Antonia.

Late the following night Paul awoke to find Jesus standing beside him. Jesus spoke words of encouragement to Paul just like He had at Corinth so long ago. He told Paul that he would be called on to go all the way to Rome with the message he preached in Jerusalem. With that Paul rested and knew that his death was not imminent.

The next morning a small band of men prepared to kill Paul. They vowed to fast until he was dead, and told the Sanhedrin council to call for him to be re-examined. Their plan was to kill him on the way to the meeting, but Paul was warned by his nephew and relayed the plot to Lysias. The captain sent a large contingent of soldiers with Paul under protective custody (accompanied by a letter that explained his actions) to the seat of the Roman Procurator named Felix at the port city of Caesarea. In his letter he explained that he saw no reason to hold Paul, but felt the need to protect him as a Roman citizen. Paul was taken away by way of Antipatris and eventually to Caesarea for an audience with Felix. Felix ordered him held and said he would hear the matter when his accusers were assembled. [Chapter 23]

Five days later, the High Priest Ananias and a delegation came from Jerusalem, together with their lawyer Tertullus. The lawyer indicated (after am extremely complimentary opening) that Paul was a seditious fellow, spreading insurrection among Jews and desiring to defile the Temple. He argued that Paul would have been killed under Jewish law had they not been disrupted by Roman guards. Paul got an opportunity to answer the charges.

His points were clear and simple. He said he had only been in Jerusalem twelve days ago, and there was no evidence of him having any dispute, raising any issue in the Temple or in any local synagogue. He argued they lacked evidence because their charges were false. He then restated for the record that he considered himself Jewish and kept the Torah law as was common to Jews in Jerusalem, but was being persecuted because he believed in the resurrection of the dead. Felix decided to wait on the arrival of Claudius Lucias to see if his testimony would clarify the accounts. In the end, Felix called for Paul to explain his message on several occasions, even before his wife who was a Jewess. In the end, he left the issue for his successor, and Paul awaited judgment for two years! [Chapter 24]

After the new Procurator, Porcius Festus, came into the office, he made a trip to Jerusalem. The High Priest and a delegation met with him and requested that Paul be sent back up to Jerusalem and put back in the jurisdiction of the Temple court. Festus decline, but did offer them the opportunity to present their case anew before the judgment seat in Caesarea. Paul came before Festus and boldly charged that there was no evidence he had done anything improper under Jewish or Roman law. Festus offered to have him sent to Jerusalem and put under Temple jurisdiction and Paul appealed to Caesar (Emperor Nero) to be held under Roman law. Festus closed the case of jurisdiction by declaring that Paul had the right under Roman law to appeal to Caesar, and he had to be sent to Rome for a hearing. [Chapter 25]

During the time Paul awaited his trip to Rome, he was called on by Procurator Festus to tell his story to Herod Agrippa II and his consort Bernice. Agrippa was a Jewish client king who served under Romans. Genuinely interested, Agrippa called on Paul to give an account of himself. Paul carefully explained all that had happened to him, from the vision on the Damascus road and the message of the risen Messiah. Agrippa told Paul, "You almost have me persuaded to join the Messianics!" Agrippa admitted afterward to Festus and Bernice that Paul was guilty of nothing. He expressed, "Had Paul not made the appeal to Caesar (a matter of Roman jurisdiction) he may have been set free." [Chapter 26]

Luke and Aristarchus of Thessalonica joined Paul for the journey to Rome. The prisoner ship was under the penal supervision of an Imperial centurion named Julius. They launched out to the north, and briefly stopped in the port of Sidon, where Julius allowed Paul to refresh himself in a local friend's home. Launching from there, they sailed south of Cyprus because north winds were making travel difficult. They turned north to Myra, along the coast of Lycia.

In Myra, Julius found a large ship of Alexandria that was heading to Rome and put the prisoners on it (the ship had a total complement of 276 people). The ship left port, but had barely any wind and traveled painfully slowly along the southern coast of Asia Minor, finally crossing into the Aegean Sea to Crete, where they harbored in the southern area called the Fair Havens, near Lasea. Paul warned them it was too late in the year to attempt the journey to Rome, but the captain of the boat felt he could make it, and did not like the conditions wintering in Fair Havens. Loosing from port, the ship was caught in a strong northwesterly wind that drove the ship beyond the ability to direct the sails, so they did their best to steer west, crossing below the island of Clauda. The timbers were loosening as a result of the fierce wind strain, and the sailors tried to keep the ship together. Caught in open sea and pulled by fierce winds, they lightened the ship on the second day, but the storm did not still. Days passed and the ship was pushing toward Sicily, but the situation grew desperate.

After a long time in the terrible storm, Paul had a message sent from God by an angelic vision. He told the crew that no one would die but they would lose the ship and be grounded on a small island. Fourteen days into the storm they knew they were coming close to landfall. Sounding depths, they got as close as they dared in darkness, dropped anchor, and waited for sunrise. Some shipmen began to lower the launches, but Paul warned the Julius and his men, "Unless these men stay on the ship, you will not be saved!" Julius had his soldiers cut the ropes, and the boats dropped into the sea.

Paul urged the whole complement, in the midst of the storm to stop and eat something. He reiterated to them that no one would die, blessed God for the bread and began to eat. The crew and prisoners ate, and then cast the rest of the cargo overboard to lighten the ship. After daybreak, they took up anchors, loosed the rudder and hoisted sail. They ran the ship aground and she began to come apart. The soldiers turned to execute all the prisoners, but Julius (in order to save Paul) told all prisoners and crew to swim for shore. As the ship broke up, the whole complement swam ashore or held to pieces of the ship to arrive to shore, but no one was lost. [Chapter 27]

Soaked but safe on dry land, the ship re-gathered its crew and prisoners on the island of Melita (Malta). The local people did not speak Greek, but they did show kind hospitality. While Paul helped to gather firewood, he was bit by a poisonous snake, but shook the snake into the fire. At first, people thought he must have been a terrible criminal who was getting his justice, but when he did not swell or die, they thought him a god!

A local man named Publius offered lodging to Paul and his companions. Publius' father was dying of dysentery, and Paul healed him. As a result, after the three days the team stayed there, people kept bringing their sick to Paul for healing. People openly expressed their thanks, and gave Paul and the whole company things they needed for the journey. Their time on the island lasted three months as they awaited another transport vessel to Rome. They were put aboard a ship of Alexandria, bearing the sign of "Castor and Pollux" and sailed for Syracuse on Sicily. After a brief three-day stop, they landed at Rhegium in southern Italy. Another brief stop and they continued on the journey north to Puteoli, catching good winds and making the trip in excellent time. At Puteoli the team met some of the faith, and remained with them for a week. News of their arrival reached the area congregations, and when they began to journey toward Rome they met believers in The Appian Forum, and even more in the Three Taverns area. Paul's heart was filled with thanks as he saw what God had done to spread the message of the Gospel. When they reached Rome, all the prisoners were surrendered to the common prison, but Julius assigned a protective guard to Paul and arranged private lodging for him.

A few days after they arrived, Paul called for the Jewish leadership of the area to meet with him to explain why he had been sent there from Jerusalem. The local leadership had received no word from the Temple leadership and was totally unaware of Paul's case. Paul had the chance to explain to them the story of the good news, and he wasted no time doing so. After his message, the leaders left discussing it among themselves. Paul hired a house and remained under guard for two years in Rome. During that time, he preached and taught openly, and no one tried to stop him. [Chapter 28]

The Emphasis of the Book of Acts

The Book of Acts is a complex letter. It appears that part of the letter was written to catalogue the spread of the Gospel geographically to various people groups. Luke probably intended to offer evidence of the fulfillment Jesus' promise before His Ascension from the Mount of Olives:

"You shall be witnesses to me in Jerusalem, Judea, Samaria and to the uttermost parts of the earth" (Acts 1:8b).

The letter seems formed around this geography, with the movement of the Gospel in Jerusalem (Acts 1:1-8:3), Judea and Samaria (8:4-40) and beyond (9-28).

Within the geographical frame above, Luke also clarifies some of the key challenges faced by the early Messianic movement. He appears to systematically move between the internal and external crises of the believers. In the early stage of the narrative he mentions the frequent threats against the Messianic leaders by the Temple authorities (4:3-7; 5:17-27), which led to the stoning of one of the Messianic leaders (6:8-7:60). Later external pressures included the rampages of Saul of Tarsus that ransacked the houses of suspected believers in Jesus in a manhunt (9:1-5). In addition to the external pressures, the movement internally fought against complaints of inequity in matters of finance among its members (6:1-7), and even lying in matters of property between followers (5:1-11). The leadership struggled to define the community of believers, and attempted to reconcile the promises of the Hebrew Scriptures to the reality of the work of the Spirit in the Gentile born followers of Jesus (Acts 11:1-18; 15:1, 6-35; 21:21-25). This pressure plagued the Messianic movement throughout the period of the writings of the various letters of the Apostles to the congregations (Epistles).

Another emphasis of the letter includes an insightful narrative of the chief personalities of the leaders in the new movement. Biographical sketches are drawn from the glimpses in the letter of individuals like Peter (2:14-5:42; 9:32-11:18), Stephen (6:1-7:60), Philip (8:1-40), Barnabas (11:19-30; 13:1-14:28) and of course Paul (9:1-31,11:25-30, 12:24-14:28, 15:36-28:31). This view of the leaders is critical to our understanding, since it is often difficult to see a balanced perspective of the leaders from their writings. Many New Testament epistles address certain arguments or problems in the fledgling congregations, without giving a sufficient background of the writer. This narrative gives a cross reference to a number of their struggles, and offers context to their other writings.

One of the most critical features of the letter is the explanation of the so-called "New Covenant" and its beginnings in the Gentile world. The Hebrew Scriptures promised that a "New Covenant" was coming to the Jewish people. A careful study of the Hebrew texts of this covenant offer no hint that Gentiles would in any way be a part of the plan. In fact, the covenant as it is described in the Hebrew Scriptures is primarily about the return of the people to the land and their hearts to the God of Abraham (Jer. 31:27-40; 32:37-40; Isa. 59:20-21; Ezek. 16:60-63, 37:21-28). One of the specific purposes of the letter to Theophilus appears to explain that while this is completely true, it was not complete. The New Covenant, according to Luke, BEGAN with a small number of Jews (cp. Acts 1 and 2), then entailed a dramatic conversion of many Gentiles (Acts 10:28-29) and would eventually END with the fulfillment of a kingdom of Jews that knew their Messiah (Acts 2:17-21). The expansion of the New Covenant to include the Gentile was probably the dominant theme in the latter half of the letter.

Finally, there is ample evidence the letter intended to offer a new and expanded explanation of the nature of the God of Abraham. Since the world of the Jews was thoroughly monotheistic, the letter attempted to offer some small explanation to the Messianic view of God. This view was an expansion of the traditional Jewish approach, not an attempt to depart from it. The view of the Hebrew text was simply that God is One. The view of the Messianic believers was that the one and only true God revealed Himself in a variety of personality roles. Each personality role was complete: independent in intellect, emotion and will. In that way, the one God was multiple in personality, but, in contrast to paganism, God was not multiple in essence – thus an extension of the essential Hebrew monotheism. The difference may appear slight, but to the Apostles it was the marking line between a pagan view, and the view consistent with the Hebrew Scriptures, which they viewed to be the exclusively true Word of God. Examples of this appear in the letter as in the case of the personification of the Holy Spirit (Acts 1:2, 5, 8), the Heavenly Father (1:4) and the obedient Son (2:27). Special emphasis in the sermons of the Apostles showed a distinction of personality between each of the three (Acts 2:32-33). In that way, the Messianic movement believed that their approach offered an expanded view of the God of Abraham.

Part Two: A Harmony of the Life and Writings of Paul in the New Testament

The remainder of these studies will very likely seem a bit different in style of writing and essential substance – because they are intentionally designed to do more than offer background – they are designed to challenge our lives as followers of Jesus based on what we learn from the New Testament record.

The following lessons are essentially Bible studies that, if successful, will move a learner through the Book of Acts along with the thirteen epistles that have Paul's "signature" in the New Testament in an historical sequence, and offer personal application to the text along the way.

Tackling the New Testament as a reference tool or history book belies the real purpose of the ancient text. **This is the story of how God did a work in the first century**, and laid the foundation of mission outreach in a world that fully embraced pagan thinking. This is also a story of how a man was shaped for a special leadership ministry that required toughness in the face of trouble and tenderness in deportment before people – even when they had stones in their hands.

The lessons in this volume recap the first half of Paul's training and journeys. Another volume follows to complete the task. The essential lessons of development are in the coming pages. They represent a "becoming the Apostle Paul" segment on growth and change, as Paul the student moves to Paul the radical. His stride utterly broken by God, Paul was led into the faith by the hand, and then sculpted by God's hand in a series of eight hard–hitting experiences. That "training ground" was unfolded in the Book of Acts and corresponding New Testament works in eight steps explained in the pages to follow:

- Paul's Conversion: A life interrupted.
- First Steps of Faith – Paul learns baby steps in Christ.
- False Start – Paul learned his natural ability wasn't the key to his future.
- Joining a Team – Paul learned the need and earned the confidence of others.
- The First Project – Paul learned about expectations amid the journey of life.
- Fight rules – Paul sat in a room with Spirit-filled men and watched Godliness amid disagreement.
- Dark Days – Paul learned to trust God instead of his eyes and experiences.
- A Letter from Rehab – Paul began his writing career for God while healing from a crushing time.

Paul's Response to the Roman World: "Paul is Converted: A Life Interrupted"

God doesn't look at people the way we do, and that is a good thing. When we look at people, we are culturally trained to *judge* them, more or less, by a set of ingrained values, many of which we may not even be consciously aware. If we see a very large person, we may immediately judge them to be undisciplined and even slovenly adorned – though the truth may be that they have a genetic disorder or a disease causing gross inflammation. We may write them off if we are looking for a "high energy go-getter type." If we see someone who is dressed in a disheveled manner, or even mismatched in their clothing, we may judge them to be a "have not" from society's lowest place – though they may actually be quite well off and just a person who does not care about fashion a whit. When we see someone exceptionally pretty or handsome by whatever the fleeting standard of our day, we are culturally cued to draw near to them and want them to approve of us or accept us. These things are ingrained from a very young age, and they are at work in virtually every interaction of your life. Some sociologists term this "cultural value stamping."

Fortunately, God is not from where I grew up. He doesn't reside in one culture, and His evaluations are not all based on my appearance, nor my past performance, but rather He relies on His ability to know **what I will become** with His transforming hand. God is at work in people that want Him to be – but so much more. He is working in the backdrop of the scenery of your life even before you are aware of Him... Such a truth can be dramatically illustrated in the life of the church history hero – Saul of Tarsus. God saw what few others could see – and God used him dramatically... but only after God forcibly interrupted Saul's life with a flash of blinding light.

Key Principle: The biggest factor that determines our life's destination is not our past or even our personality – but our willingness to embrace God's change in us and control over us.

A few years ago, I picked up a book entitled <u>When People are Big and God is Small</u> by Edward Welch. I didn't read the book, because I was so struck by its title. I began to think about that and put the book back on the rack. What a great title! Have you gone through a time in your life when you made God too small in your eyes, and made people too important? That seems to summarize the setting of the beginning of the story of a companion I have been sharing my life with over the past thirty years. In my obsessive desire to know the Bible, I traveled through almost all the places identified by church historians as part of the life of the Apostle Paul. In this series of lessons, I want to walk through that journey with you.

I want you to meet my friend back where he began. He was a good guy, well educated, properly spoken and sharply adorned. He came from a good family, and got a first-class education. He was a free Roman and a Jew. He had a Latin mind for organization, a Greek tongue for the study of human wisdom, and a Hebrew heart to know God – the perfect combination for the task that God outlined for his life. Though this story is about him, and not you, it is worth remembering that **you are, in fact, genetically perfect for the task God has assigned to you**. He knows what He needs and He made you because you are needed in the intricate tapestry of God's full plan to make Himself known.

The first time we meet my friend, he was standing with his university friends in Jerusalem and listening to a speaker that was systematically alienating and aggravating the crowd surrounding him. The speaker's name was Stephen, and the subject of his prolonged lecture was the defense of God's work through Jesus of Nazareth – a life changing influence that was changing people in Jerusalem's Jewish community by the thousands, and was becoming a source of profound aggravation to the Judean aristocracy in general, and the Temple leadership in particular. The scene was recorded in Acts 7, and it was quite tense, the air filled with a combination of hot, dry dust and bitter-tasting anger:

*Acts 7:54 Now when they heard this, (referring to Stephen's apologetic preaching) they were cut to the quick, and they [began] gnashing their teeth at him. 55 But being full of the Holy Spirit, he gazed intently into heaven and saw the glory of God, and Jesus standing at the right hand of God; 56 and he said, "Behold, I see the heavens opened up and the Son of Man standing at the right hand of God." 57 But they **cried out with a loud voice**, and **covered their ears** and **rushed at him** with one impulse. 58 When they had **driven him out of the city**, they [began] stoning [him]; and the witnesses laid aside their robes at the feet of a young man named Saul.*

Freeze the movie frame there. Here was the auspicious beginning scene for Saul who would become the most accomplished writer among the Apostles. Could you see it? Of course not! He was one of the crowd – nothing more outstanding could be said of him than the fact that people trusted him with their robes while the stoned a man to death. But wait... that isn't **NOTHING**. Saul was a man in whom others placed confidence. They left their valuables with him. They may have sounded like radicals, and certainly they were – but **Saul was a trusted radical in their midst. He served them, and that made him both notable and trusted**. Don't forget the way to importance is always by serving the needs of others – it was an early lesson Saul seemed to get. Let's move back into the scene...

Acts 7:59 They went on stoning Stephen as he called on [the Lord] and said, "Lord Jesus, receive my spirit!" 60 Then falling on his knees, he cried out with a loud voice, "Lord, do not hold this sin against them!" Having

*said this, he fell asleep. Acts 8:1 Saul was in **hearty
agreement** with putting him to death. And on **that day a
great persecution began against the church in
Jerusalem**, and they were all **scattered** throughout the
regions of Judea and Samaria, except the apostles. 2
[Some] devout men buried Stephen, and made loud
lamentation over him. 3 But **Saul [began] ravaging the
church**, **entering house after house**, and **dragging** off
men and women, he would **put them in prison**. 4
Therefore, those who had been scattered went about
preaching the word...*

The text shifted quickly, as the storm against the Jerusalem
church seemed to grow to a "flash point" in almost a moment. A
trusted young man was holding the coats in one scene, and was
leading the charge into the home of unsuspecting followers of
Jesus in the next. Who was this man? We are fortunate,
because we have an answer. Because he wrote thirteen letters
of the New Testament that are specifically accepted by scholars
as from his quill (or his traveling secretarial companions), we
know a good bit about the man. I want to introduce him the way
he later introduced himself in many scriptures.

The Uniqueness of Paul

I think it is fair to say that Saul of Tarsus was a unique man,
chosen for a very special mission. In fact, Acts 1:23 shares the
details of how the Apostles chose a successor to Judas Iscariot.
Essentially the choice came down to two men: Joseph called
Barsabbas (surnamed Justus) and a follower of Jesus known as
Matthais. The latter (Matthais) was chosen, but was **never
heard about again in the writings of the Christian
Scriptures**. Some argue the leaders may have been "out of step
with God" (though the narrative does not appear to be a
statement of disobedience). One thing is *certain*, waiting in the
wings for a Divine meeting was "Shaul of Tarsus" whose
conversion and writings would powerfully impact the disciples
from the first century until now (as we will see in our study of
Acts 9 and beyond). Scholars have argued that **Paul was
unique in the record in five ways**.

First, Paul was the most **controversial** man among the early leaders. The record of Church History reveals that he was called an **"illegitimate charlatan" by Pseudo Clement**, but highly regarded by others. He was widely followed and bitterly disputed all at the same time. In other words, he was a dynamic leader!

Second was the noted and incredible "expansive view" of Paul – he was a **visionary** in many ways unique to his time and place. Though Jesus spoke mainly to Jews and called on them to follow their King, Paul (by the direction of the Holy Spirit) recognized the expanded definition of "spiritual kingdom" – stretching that definition even into the Gentile world. He recognized the shifted pattern of God's work, and followed after the movement of the Spirit. His chief argument with the other leaders was that the Spirit **indicated a change in the direction of the outreach** (Gal. 3:2), and the church must follow that direction. He saw it well before most of his peers (cp. Acts 15) and **argued when he saw a conflict in the leadership over the new direction** (Gal. 2:1ff).

Third, a uniqueness of the "Apostle to the Gentiles" (as he called himself in Rom. 11:13) can be seen in the way God used him to communicate **revolutionary** new ideas to the young churches. Paul "broke ground" on a number issues: divorce, inter-ethnic marriage, acceptable styles of dress in worship, the public behavior of women particularly in ministry, family issues, and eschatology (particularly issues like our "resurrection bodies", etc). His use of the holy principles of the Hebrew Scriptures and the revelation offered to the church by the Spirit through his pen offered the window not only into the Roman world and its problems, but into the method and principles of problem solving for the church of every age!

Though often thought of as a domineering leader (perhaps because of some very hard words to the Corinthian Church), a fourth uniqueness of Paul was that he was actually extremely **relational** and caring. He openly praised the good in others (Phil. 1) and thought of the people of God as related in every way. It is no accident that the Spirit of God used Paul to explain the **"body concept"** of the church, with Messiah as the Head (1

Cor. 12:12ff). He obviously felt that his life was an example to believers everywhere (Phil. 3:4ff) and expressed deep emotion in his dealings with their sin and troubles (2 Cor. 2:4; Phil. 4:1). The closing words from his quill were all about the people in his life, not simply a sterile list of accomplishments (2 Timothy 4).

Finally, a fifth way Paul was unique in the early leadership of the church - he was uniquely **exposed**. Though we have other records about the foundations of the church and its leaders, we have nothing so complete as the record of and by Paul. Though the four Gospels offer a reasonably complete picture of Jesus, we have no physical writings of Jesus. In the case of Paul, we have both the writings about him (i.e. the Book of Acts) and the letters written by him to the young churches and leaders.

Paul's Background

The essential facts about Paul's life are, for the most part, documented in the Christian Scriptures by the man's own letters. At the same time, these facts are but a **shadow of the man** that stood the test of brutal beatings, shipwrecks, homeless wanderings and many rejections for the cause of proclaiming Jesus. Let's set up our series of lessons with some significant things about Paul that we know.

First, we know something about his various **names**. He was named at his circumcision after the first king of Israel ('Shaul'). Bible students recall that King Saul was selected by his peers in part because of his physical stature. He was known as the king that stood "a head above" other men of his day, and that appealed to the insecure Israelite tribal leaders. In contrast, the Apostle Paul was short in stature. A possible reference to this was his Gentile name "Paulus" which loosely has been translated as "short, stubby one." Though some writers and Bible teachers unfamiliar with Jewish customs offer the notion that Saul was the "unregenerate" name of the Apostle, Paul did not exchange one name for another after his conversion. On the contrary, every Jew of the diaspora was traditionally named according the formula, "And his name shall be named among the Jews as ___, but among the Gentiles he shall be called

____." Saul possessed both names from the time of his parent's naming ceremony. We have become accustomed to calling him by the "name among the Gentiles" because most of the ministry record we have comes from the time of his service outside the land of Israel, among the Gentiles that came to faith. It is worth noting that his size and name left little restriction on his impact. John Chrysostom, (c. 345-407) a leader of the Byzantine Church is quoted as saying, **"He was barely five feet tall, with a reach that touched the stars."**

In addition to the knowledge concerning his names, we surmise the **birth date** of Paul to be about 5 CE, during the end of the reign of Caesar Augustus (who ruled until the year 14 CE). It is **certain** that he was born during the first decade of the first century, making him a younger contemporary to Jesus. By the Scriptural record, we know that Paul never met Jesus before the Savior's Resurrection and he was still "a young man" (Acts 7:58, a reference to his early thirties) at the time he was "holding the cloaks" at the stoning of Stephen in Jerusalem.

Paul's **hometown** was the city of Tarsus, and he seemed quite proud of that fact. He apparently liked his "home teams" and mentioned his home – the place of the third largest "university city" in the empire (behind Alexandria and Rome) whenever he got the chance. (Acts 7:58; 9:11, 30; 11:25; 21:39; 22:3; 22:28; 26:9-10; Rom. 11:1; 2 Cor. 11:22; Gal. 1:14; Phil. 3:4-7; 2 Tim. 3:14ff). Some scholars speculate that Paul may be a descendant of some of those who were promised free citizenship if they moved to the Cilician city in 171 BCE. Another claim for the citizenship ancestry of Paul can be found in some who raise the possibility that Paul's father or grandfather helped Marc Antony (and thus Rome) during Cleopatra's renowned visit to Tarsus in 41 BCE. The historian Strabo mentions the splendor of the event, as Cleopatra sailed her gilded barge in the Cyndus River into the city. In addition, there is reason to believe that Antony and Octavian used some resources of the city in their struggle against Brutus and Cassius, who they later defeated at Philippi in Macedonia. Some have even suggested that a tent maker's gift could have been repaid in citizenship (cp. Acts 18:3), though this is mere speculation.

In addition to being the hometown of Paul (Acts 9:11; 21:39; 22:3), it was also the city Paul returned to after his escape from Jerusalem (Acts 9:30). **Barnabas found Paul in the city and enlisted him to service at Antioch** (Acts 11:25ff). Paul may well have **visited on the Second and Third Mission Journeys** (Acts 15:41; 18:22-23). Paul was proud of this important city (Acts 21:39) and his free citizenry, a sentiment common to Roman citizens who often had significant rivalries between cities in athletics, etc.

Paul's **occupation** was also recorded in the Bible (Acts 18:3, 20:34; 1 Cor. 4:12) as that of a tentmaker or leather worker. The Greek term "Skenopoios" was used to refer to a variety of binding and weaving crafts. The area of Cilicia, the region of Tarsus, was noted in antiquity for the quality goat hair tents (called "cilicum"). Some scholars even suggest that Paul's family may have secured citizenship by providing tents to the Roman army during the transition from Republic to Empire.

Students of the Bible can also reasonably identify the key elements to the **education** of the Apostle Paul. His early life in Tarsus was no doubt impacted by the university in town that was legendary in the time. When he moved to Jerusalem and out of the shadow of the university, Paul studied under the moderate Pharisaic instructor Gamaliel (Acts 22:3). He was learned enough to become a Pharisee (Acts 23:6). His quotations of the Hebrew Scriptures are usually from the Septuagint version (250 BCE), a possible sign that his memorization of the Word was done from the Greek translation. He apparently could speak the Hebrew language (Phil. 3:5; Acts 21:40) and Greek (Acts 21:37) and perhaps Latin (though this is not certain).

Near to the heart of any Jew of antiquity was his **tribe** affiliation. Paul was of the tribe of Benjamin, the ancient possessors of the heartland of Israel. The area of the hill country is north of Jerusalem and is centered on the ridge route of the Patriarchs and Matriarchs. The territory was the dwelling of King Saul of old, and included such important Biblical places as Gibeon,

Bethel, Ai, Mizpah, and Shiloh (the place the Tabernacle was placed for much of the pre-Temple times.

We know only a few things about Paul's **family**. By his own admission he was brought up by observant Jewish parents in the diaspora (i.e. "son of a Pharisee" – cp. Acts 23:6). He no doubt had a number of brothers and sisters, but **only mentions one sister indirectly in Acts 23:16**. He alluded to his father on a few occasions, but never made any mention of his mother in any of his epistles (see Rom. 16).

Paul's **successes** are also well known. He has been called a fanatic (defined as "**he can't change his mind, and he can't change the subject!**"). He was usually followed by a riot or a revival! Yet, one third of the Christian Scriptures were written at his hand. We know of fourteen and possess now thirteen letters to young churches and pastors, but there were no doubt others. His style was **sometimes complex** enough to draw the observation by Peter "some of Paul's words are hard to understand!" (2 Peter 3:15-16). In addition to his writings, his energetic travel schedule took him to more on journeys totaling more than **10,000 miles**.

His **travels** were often met by troubles (Acts 16:22) and he was asked to leave on a number of occasions (as in Acts 16:39). We have only a traditional record of his **death**. The "Apocryphal Acts of Paul" (a dubious source in many respects) offers the detail that Paul was beheaded along a main shopping district on the west side of Rome at the hand of the executioners of Emperor Nero in 67 CE.

The broad view

Step back for moment and look at a quick overview of an important man God used in all our lives. He was saved in 36 CE at about age 31 or 32, and died in the year 67 or 68 CE at age 62 or 63. **Half his life he followed a zealous religious life, and then he met God's Son. His was a life interrupted by God's grace**. With only half of his life left – he accomplished more than any other of his day. How? The answer is found again in the Scriptures, back in the record of the Book of Acts, chapter 9.

9:1 Now Saul, still breathing threats and murder against the disciples of the Lord, went to the high priest, 2 and asked for letters from him to the synagogues at Damascus, so that if he found any belonging to the Way, both men and women, he might bring them bound to Jerusalem. 3 As he was traveling, it happened that he was approaching Damascus, and suddenly a light from heaven flashed around him; 4 and he fell to the ground and heard a voice saying to him, "Saul, Saul, why are you persecuting Me?" 5 And he said, "Who are You, Lord?" And He [said], **"I am Jesus whom you are persecuting,** *6 but get up and enter the city, and it will be told you what you must do." 7 The men who traveled with him stood speechless, hearing the voice but seeing no one. 8* **Saul got up from the ground, and though his eyes were open, he could see nothing; and leading him by the hand, they brought him into Damascus.**

In 9:1 we begin the paragraph with Saul looking powerful and menacing – but all this suddenly changed. A flash of light, a voice from on high, and the youthful and ardent stride of Saul was broken forever. He started the passage looking ahead at life, but when he met Jesus, he found out that he couldn't really see at all. The journey that began with him in the lead, ended with him being led by the hand, unable to see the turns in the bumpy road.

As we study the life and ministry of Saul or Tarsus, don't venerate the man. He was as frail as any other, and as subject to the sin nature as all of us. Yet, from the encounter with Jesus onward, the man learned a secret... The interruption of his life became his greatest blessing. The unexpected call of God became the driving force of his life. Saul FELL INTO GOD'S GRACE, and that was a powerful place to be.

Saul's Secret

Saul's greatest power lay not in his ability, but in his surrender of all his life choices to serve his King, his Lord – his Master. Falling into grace was God's work of introduction, but growing in grace (as he later told Timothy to do in 2 Timothy 2:1) required the deliberate withdrawal of control of life's choices to the direction of God's Spirit under the Lordship or mastery of Jesus Christ. Philippians 3 says it in his own words: "...beware of the false circumcision; 3 ...and put no confidence in the flesh, 4 ... If anyone else has a mind to put confidence in the flesh, I far more: 5 circumcised the eighth day, of the nation of Israel, of the tribe of Benjamin, a Hebrew of Hebrews; as to the Law, a Pharisee; 6 as to zeal, a persecutor of the church; as to the righteousness which is in the Law, found blameless. 7 But whatever things were gain to me, those things I have counted as loss for the sake of Christ. 8 More than that, I count all things to be loss in view of the surpassing value of knowing **Christ Jesus my Lord**...

Saul didn't consider Jesus simply as his Friend, or his Helpful Guide – but rather as his "KURIOS" – his Master. Jesus called the shots on Saul's life. When we move ahead in the story, Jesus will be at every turn in the road of Saul's life, directing him, guiding him and commanding him. It started with Jesus' appearance to Ananias in Damascus to accept Saul and help him grow... but it goes on and on in the story. In every story we will see God at work directing... but that isn't the key to the story. God is doing that in all of us. He isn't silent... He just isn't finding many that are willing to listen and surrender.

The secret of Saul was his decision – his final determination that **his life was not his own** - period. Because he didn't see his life as his own, God could direct him and use him. He didn't find it in religion – he found it when he met and surrendered his life to Jesus on a roadway. GK Chesterton was right when he wrote: "The mark of faith is not **tradition**, but **conversion**. It is the

miracle by which men find truth *in spite of tradition* and often with the rending of all the roots of humanity."

His secret was that he met God, and took God's mastery of his life seriously. The same can be said of you. **The biggest factor that determines our life's destination is not our past or even our personality – but our willingness to embrace God's change in us and control over us.**

Paul's Response to the Roman World: "New Faith: Learning for the First Time, All over again!"

When I walked into her room, I knew she was **changed** from the woman I had come to know over the years. The first sign was the **missing smile** from her face, and the second the lack of her unusually **boisterous voice** saying, "Well if it isn't the preacher man!" No, this time she sat in silence, with barely the ability to move her face at all. The stroke attacked all her functions, but left her in the frustrating state of **full-minded imprisonment**. She could think, but not speak; she could process but not deliver. In the months that followed, one by one, her brain was retrained to learn things all over again – things we don't even think about doing anymore. She once told me that she was "**learning things for the first time all over again!**" – I knew exactly what she meant as I watched her do each...

I mention my old friend because her story illustrates in the **physical realm** what happened long ago to Saul of Tarsus in the spiritual realm. In fact, and many of us went through in our first "**growing steps" of faith in Christ** learning life all over again. Though his story was nearly two thousand years ago, his conversion was **not dissimilar** to many people I know. They may not have been "struck down on the road to Damascus", but **God cut deeply into their broken lives** – and they weren't ready for what God wanted to change. Let me see if by looking at Saul's early steps, we can see more clearly the struggle, and then allow God to make sense of His solution to the issue.

Go back in our story and observe Saul the day **BEFORE** he met Jesus on the road. He was a **competent** and **capable** student of the Word of God, and he was a **zealous** follower of Temple politics. He had gained the confidence of his fellows early, and used that to build a **reputation** that was formidable. He exhibited neither laziness nor dull minded slowness – but **none**

of those attributes made him a re-born child of God. He was enthusiastic and zealous, but lost in self-moved and self-measured religion. At the moment of the apogee of his human influence, Jesus cut him down on the roadway, and his life was forever changed. By the end of that conversion story (where we left him in our last lesson) he was blind, hungry and separated from those who understood his past or could perceive his incredible destiny. What happened next is the story of this lesson – **the "first steps" of new faith**…Yet there is a single principle underlying the text that we must bear in mind…

Key Principles: Some of the initial lessons of faith are the hardest simply because they set the expectation for the rest of our time of service to the King.

Seven Lessons for the "New Beginning"

Paul faced an entire change in his life – one that moved him from an enemy of the Cross to a follower of the Savior. Few men in recorded history have such a radical transformative event, and yet literally millions understand what happened to Paul. They may not have had their lives documented, but they understand the radical changes that come into a life interrupted by God's grace. Having lived a dramatic life before his Christ encounter, Acts 9 opens up eight critical lessons that Paul needed to learn to help set the tone and expectation for his life "in Christ". Don't skip by these lessons, for they are not mere "place holders" in the story. Our expectations weigh heavily in our walk – for those who don't learn what to expect can easily be drawn off course in discouragement when their false ideas are not confirmed.

Lesson One: God doesn't always remove troubles instantly – because He works through difficult circumstances (Acts 9:8-9).

The first lesson that Saul needed to confront is found in these two simple verses:

Acts 9:8 Saul got up from the ground, and though his eyes were open, he could see nothing; and leading him by the hand, they brought him into Damascus. 9 And he was three days without sight, and neither ate nor drank.

Ironically, God blinded Saul so that he could get him to see the truth about life. God had an incredible plan for Saul's life, but a man so competent couldn't simply bound his way into that plan on his own power and with his own abilities. In fact, God could only get Saul to move forward by forcing him to a "dead stop".

God didn't just make him helpless... He left him in that state for three long days and nights. On the back side of the narrative that may not sound like a long time, but in the midst of it, Saul had no idea that this wasn't going to be his "new normal" – and his whole life wasn't about to unravel. There is no way Saul could be happy in darkness - but in the midst of the trouble, Saul could learn the meaning of JOY. **Happiness is about what I am going through, while joy is about Who I am trusting as I pass through it.**

Dwight L. Moody said it well, "Happiness is caused by things that happen **around** me, and circumstances will mar it; but joy flows right on through trouble; joy flows on through the dark; joy flows in the night as well as in the day; joy flows all through persecution and opposition. It is an unceasing fountain bubbling up in the heart; a secret spring the world can't see and doesn't know anything about." [SOURCE: Dwight Lyman Moody as quoted by Edythe Draper, Draper's Book of Quotations for the Christian World (Wheaton: Tyndale House Publishers, Inc., 1992).

Saul needed to learn to trust God and not the circumstances – but he needed something even DEEPER – a lesson many have forgotten. God is not cruel when He delays respite from trouble. He has a purpose that is perfectly timed and properly placed into your life. You may not think so, but that is one way we can learn that we are not God. He is not a genie in our bottle, but a Creator, Sustainer and Master. I am the needy, He is the Knowing One. Trust will always be an issue if I don't learn early that God does not use my watch to operate His Kingdom. That was the point of the three days and nights...

Here is the point: Either God gets to be God or He doesn't. Either He chooses my path and I follow His lead, or I am faking the Christian life and trying to lead the dance of life. Saul needed that lesson – but so do we all.

Lesson Two: Your mission from God will require the involvement of others – because God works through teams (Acts 9:10-12).

A second lesson was also in order:

Acts 9:10 Now there was a disciple at Damascus named Ananias; and the Lord said to him in a vision, "Ananias." And he said, "Here I am, Lord." 11 And the Lord [said] to him, "Get up and go to the street called Straight, and inquire at the house of Judas for a man from Tarsus named Saul, for he is praying, 12 and he has seen in a vision a man named Ananias come in and lay his hands on him, so that he might regain his sight."

It is easy for gifted, talented and capable Christians to miss the need for others – and it is a deep lesson we all need to take to heart. A few years ago, Galen Clark wrote this commentary about team members that I clipped out: "Richie Incognito and Jonathan Martin had every reason as teammates to be friends, but they were not. Incognito harassed and bullied Martin. He called him a racial slur in a voicemail played by every media outlet in the country. He threatened to kill him and his family.

Incognito claimed all of this was just locker room talk. It is the way the guys talk to one another in the NFL. Apparently, Martin didn't get the memo. Martin left his lucrative job citing emotional issues and fearing for his life. Though we don't know all the details, it appears as if Martin has some culpability, as well. He was far too passive in dealing with Incognito's threatening behavior. As a teammate, it appears, he should have expressed how troubling Incognito's threats were to him. These two men had many more reasons to get along than to have a toxic relationship. Consider all the reasons they had to be friends. They were both football players. On the same team. Had the same coach. Both were offensive linemen. Both played on the same side of the line. Both were starters. Both wanted to win. Both are big dudes. Both were millionaires. Yet somewhere along the way one or both of them forgot they played for the same team and began to treat the other like a New England Patriot. They forgot the enemy was in another city. They forgot enemy is on another team. How often I have heard Christian conversation that seemed like brothers forgot where the battle truly can be found. Strong leaders need to be especially careful of the way they learn their need for others.

This past week I participated in a forum on doctrine for the fellowship of churches to which I belong. Men came together from across the country, and hours of discussions produced a newly affirmed doctrinal framework for our churches as we face the emerging issues of our time with renewed vigor and hope. It was a lively discussion with men who love Jesus and yet found themselves quite different from one another. All of us were called by One Lord, but we all felt drawn to specific issues and emphases in ministry – based on the path Jesus placed before us. Gathering together in one room, the energy of team and the gentle reasonableness of maturity overcame what could have been a very negative experience. I will not soon forget how positive this experience was for all of us.

One of the men that impressed me deeply was a long-time friend and fellow Pastor from a Pennsylvania church that tried (sometimes in vain) to "chair" the meeting. He was kind to all of us, careful in his speech, and affirming in his words. Yet, he had conviction in his voice and firmness in his words. I was encouraged by the combination.

Saul needed to learn to temper his voice with those God would place on his team. It isn't always easy – especially when we are used to being the leading voice in the room. At the same time, it is an absolutely essential lesson – **we cannot, we will not and we must not work alone in the Kingdom**. Sometimes we have to go a long way to help people know we understand where they are coming from, and that we love them in spite of our differences.

Fred Parsons wrote many years ago a little story that makes the point: A grandfather found his grandson, jumping up and down in his playpen, crying at the top of his voice. When Johnnie saw his grandfather, he reached up his little chubby hands and said, "Out, Gramp, out." It was only natural for Grandfather to reach down to lift the little fellow out of his predicament; but as he did, the mother of the child stepped up and said, "No, Johnnie, you are being punished, so you must stay in." The grandfather was at a loss to know what to do. The child's tears and chubby hands reached deep into his heart, but the mother's firmness in correcting her son for misbehavior must not be lightly taken. Here was a problem of love versus law, but love found a way. The grandfather could not take the youngster out of the playpen, so he crawled in with him.

Sometimes the best way to show love is identify with the plight of another. It doesn't rescue them, but it does give them comradery in the trouble! Seriously, Saul needed to learn the value of the team.

Lesson Three: Though your sin is forgiven, some troubles will still follow you – because uses even our weakness to grow us to full stature in Christ (Acts 9:13-14).

A third lesson was just as essential:

> Acts 9:13 But Ananias answered, "Lord, I have heard from many about this man, how much harm he did to Your saints at Jerusalem; 14 and here he has authority from the chief priests to bind all who call on Your name."

The verses are clear – Saul was a known quantity in Ananias' life, and not a desired one. The fact is that our reputation is forged over the long haul, and God's forgiveness doesn't automatically equal man's forgiveness. If we were poor parents before we came to Christ, our adult children may not greet our new faith with open arms. We sinned against THEM as well, and that will take time to repair – if it can be this side of heaven. I doubt that Saul would have been fully embraced by Stephen's family the first week of his new faith.

We all WANT to forgive people – but we have to admit it isn't all that easy to do when the hurt was deep. Don't take Ananias' words too lightly. He wrestled with God because he didn't KNOW if Saul was sincere in a change of heart.

Look at his words. "Lord, I know about this guy!" Was he implying that God didn't? I don't think so. I believe what he was doing was making clear something that Luke included in the text for a specific lesson to the church – When "all things become new" (2 Corinthians 5:17) for the believer the reference primarily concerns our state before God. The mortgage company doesn't forgive our debts and our waist line doesn't automatically shrink to a manageable and healthy level. Things that took a long time to break will take a long time to fix – unless God decides to chop into the norm with a miracle. He can – but often He chooses to let us learn to work our way back out of the problem. It is in working through our problems that God builds our strength, and teaches us patience for one another. After all, all the believers around you have their own dragons of the past to slay.

We make a terrible mistake when we try to apply the benefits of our "new life in Christ" to some **guarantee** that repairs to injured relationships and physical damage from poor habits will be either immediately healed or easily righted. God didn't say that – poorly educated televangelists did. Real healing takes real work and real time. God can do it instantly, but that shouldn't be our expectation – or we may set ourselves up for deep disappointment.

Lesson Four: God's choice of you trumps any deficiencies you bring to the mission – because God chose the best vessel for the work He called you to (Acts 9:15).

Fortunately, for the last lesson, there is a balancing truth, found in the next verse...

*Acts 9:15 But the Lord said to him, "Go, for he is a **chosen** instrument of Mine, to bear My name before the Gentiles and kings and the sons of Israel;*

Take a deep breath... God chose you. He knew what He was getting better than you knew what you were giving Him. He made you. You are genetically perfect for God's call in your life. You aren't from the wrong side of the tracks – but from exactly where you needed to be from to help you think the way you do. God has a chosen path for His children – and your job isn't to invent it, it is to FIND IT.

It is ironic that Saul wasn't the one learning this lesson in the text... Ananias was! Saul, like many great leaders, likely sensed

God's hand in his life. At the same time, Dr. Luke (the writer of the account) made clear that is what God told Ananias. God essentially said: "I've got BIG PLANS for Saul!" Go wanted to march him into places of power and give him the task to speaking truth to powerful men and women. His job wasn't going to be easy.

Not to step off this lesson at all, but consider this: God is preparing in our midst some of the children and youths that will tackle the next great challenge of the Kingdom. We dare not take nursery duty lightly! Sunday School must be prepared well. Children's ministry must include Godly models! Youth must be drawn into the study of God's Word at the deepest level we are able to give them. The days ahead will require confidence and knowledge of the Word of God, and we must train them – for they also are chosen instruments of our Master.

Lesson Five: God's plan for you may include living through times that are very uncomfortable for you – because God's plan is set in a battle to redeem a fallen world (Acts 9:16).

A fifth lesson is both powerful, and in some ways, troublesome...

Acts 9:16 for I will show him how much he must suffer for My name's sake."

Consider how clear God was on the coming troubles for Saul of Tarsus. Why? Why didn't God clear the path of trouble if He loved Saul and wanted his mission to succeed? Those are loaded questions. The truth is that there are a number of reasons – but one of them is that Saul needed to learn to trust God THROUGH the troubles, not just recognize that God was greater than his troubles. Let me illustrate what I mean with the words of a woman writer:

[My daughter], Allison, came home for the weekend. She opened the door, didn't speak, and dropped her duffel bag. Smudges of mascara circled her eyes. I whispered a "God-please-no" prayer. "Come tell me about your classes." I patted the sofa. She muttered, "Gotta take a shower." As she clomped upstairs, I analyzed the recent changes in her: complaints of not having any money, rarely answers the phone, weight loss, pinpoint pupils, and a "who gives a rip" [facade]. I searched her purse and found a leopard-colored pipe and the unmistakable sweet odor of pot. My heart fluttered wildly like a bird stuck inside my chest. She plodded down the stairs, hair in a towel, wearing the same wrinkled clothes. Be still and talk in a sweet voice, I told myself. You must convince her to stop. "We need to talk, honey." "Not now. I'm tired." "I found your pipe." She stared at me with death-row eyes. "Chill, it's not that big of a deal." The tightness in the den suffocated me. I needed air. "Want to walk?" I asked brightly. "Like we used to?" "Whatever." I knew I could talk some sense into her. "Honey, please. You've gotta stop." I grabbed her hand. "Mom!" She jerked away. "We have a strong family history. You don't want to..." I never got to finish the sentence. Allison stormed out of the room and within minutes was headed back to college. I knew what I had to do--abandon everything in my life and start to worry/fix/control full-time. I began spending most days by the phone. I evaluated Allison's reactions, gestures, and comments. Thoughts circled my mind like buzzards: What if she never stops? What if I never see her again? What if she overdoses? Or goes to jail? I lured Allison into therapy by promising we'd go to an Italian restaurant before visits. Her first appointment day arrived. She played with her spaghetti, and I couldn't eat. "So, what do you plan to say to the counselor?" I asked. "How should I know?" When they called her name at the office, I hurried in to make sure the counselor understood. Allison refused to sign for me to have any information. I considered eavesdropping, but too many people were around. An hour later, she walked past me as I paid. "What'd you talk about?" "Just stuff." Our therapy/lunch charade continued that way for a few weeks. Then Allison's sister informed me she was still using. She denied it, refused to see the counselor, dropped out of college, and stopped answering my calls. I was convinced if I forgot about Allison, even for a second, or enjoyed anything, something bad might happen. Several months later, after another night of little sleep, I glanced in the mirror. I could have passed for the addict: dark circles under hopeless eyes. I called my friend Linda. Her son, also an addict, had been sentenced to state prison. "You can't imagine all that's going on here," I said. "Come over for coffee," she urged. I wanted to stand guard at home but knew she'd listen and understand. "Hey, girlfriend." Linda hugged me. I didn't touch my coffee as I blurted the saga. Linda didn't sweet-talk. "You need help." "You haven't heard the whole story," I argued. "I'm fine--my daughter, she needs help." "You're addicted to worry and control," Linda said. "I've been where you are." She stretched out on the sofa. "The only one you can control is yourself." The possibility that she might be right terrified me. "It took me years to realize that I'm not in charge. God is," Linda admitted. "By worrying, you're telling God he can't handle things. Go to Al-Anon with me." I'd heard of Al-Anon but didn't see how it applied to me. But I agreed because I was in awe of Linda. I didn't open my mouth during the meeting. Every word spoken sounded like my own thoughts: "I worried myself sick about my alcoholic husband." "My peace comes only when I let go and let God." Then the speaker said, "To change, you'll have to leave behind some familiar lifelong habits." But how? This is who I am--what I do. "An alcoholic can't drink, and those of us in this room can't allow an ounce of worry. For us, it's every bit as dangerous and addictive. Worry robs our serenity." I didn't think change was possible. Not for me. But I knew one thing for sure--I was destroying my life. That night at home I got real. "Help me, God. I can't do this without you." I began to ask God for help each morning. I whispered, "Not my job," as worry, fear, or control tried to needle back in. Two years after that first Al-Anon meeting, Allison and I met for an impromptu lunch. She'd gone back to the same therapist. On her own. "You can't imagine how easy it is to study when you're not high," she laughed. "Nope, I guess not." I blinked back happy tears. "Thanks, Mom." "For what?" "When you didn't fix my problems, it scared me. A few times I had to dig change out of the seat of my car for gas money. Some days," she paused, "I didn't have food." My throat felt warm with pride. She'd done it on her own. "I'm making A's. And look," she handed me her checkbook. "I have money again." Recovery defies logic. It means doing the opposite of what feels natural. When I took care of myself and my addictions, Allison did the same. Citation: Condensed from our sister publication Today's Christian,© 2008 Christianity Today International Julie W., "Not My Job," Today's Christian (July/August 2008)

Here is the bottom line of this lesson: we live in a fallen world, and the influence of the enemy is all over the place – but God is at work. He is not at work only in the GOOD THINGS of life – God is at work everywhere. The question isn't: "How do I get out of the pain and trouble?" as much as it is: "God, how can you use me in the pain and trouble? What do I need to learn from you today?"

Lesson Six: All the preparation and talent in the world isn't enough to fulfill your mission – because God's power is vested in God's Spirit (Acts 9:17).

Saul was incredibly gifted, and excelled early in life. He needed the lesson of the next two verses...

*Acts 9:17 So Ananias departed and entered the house, and after laying his hands on him said, "Brother Saul, the Lord Jesus, who appeared to you on the road by which you were coming, has sent me so that you may regain your sight and be **filled with the Holy Spirit**."*

Saul needed God's Spirit more than he needed the restoration of his physical eyesight. God was about to give him both – but the Spirit became the secret to really being able to see. God wanted Saul to see as few others could. He wanted him to evaluate things in a spiritual way. He wanted him to recognize the truth articulated well by C.S. Lewis: "You don't have a soul. You are a soul. You have a body!" No believer is truly mature until they see the physical world as many times smaller than the spiritual world that entirely engulfs the cosmos.

"In January, 1995, according to an article written by Gary Thomas, J. Robert Ashcroft had fewer than forty-eight hours to live, but he was holding on to life, hoping to see his son, John Ashcroft, sworn into the U.S. Senate the following day. [John Ashcroft, as we all know by now, is in the process of being confirmed as our next Attorney General]. As family and friends gathered in Washington for a small reception, J. Robert Ashcroft asked his son to play the piano while everyone sang, 'We Are Standing On Holy Ground.'" "After the song, the frail old man spoke some powerful words: '**John, I want you to know that even Washington can be holy ground. Wherever you hear the voice of God, that ground is sanctified. It's a place where God can call you to the highest and best.'**" "Wherever we are in our vocation, if Jesus is Lord of our lives, that place is a holy place of service for Him" (Thomas, "Working for All It's Worth," Moody, July/August 1998, p. 13, as quoted in Morgan, p. 796).

There was a man who knew that WHERE was not the question – but IN WHOSE POWER was the ultimate query. Work done by the talented will wash quickly away. Work done by the Spirit of God cannot be undone by mere mortals.

Lesson Seven: Though conversion is a spiritual act, not everything about you is spiritual – because God works through the frailty of earthen vessels (Acts 9:18).

One final lesson from our text...

Acts 9:18 And immediately there fell from his eyes something like scales, and he regained his sight, and he got up and was baptized; 19 and he took food and was strengthened.

Here is the great truth that we are but men and women. We who know God and proclaim His love, do so in earthen vessels... in cracked pots. Our bodies are not indestructible, and they need tending. We need not baby them – they also need discipline. I am heartened by this story:

One of God's faithful missionaries, Allen Gardiner, experienced many physical difficulties and hardships throughout his service to the Savior. Despite his troubles, he said, "**While God gives me strength, failure will not deter me.**" In 1851, at the age of 57, he died of disease and starvation while serving on Picton Island at the southern tip of South America. When his body was found, **his diary lay nearby**. It bore the record of hunger, thirst, wounds, and loneliness. The last entry in his little book showed the struggle of his shaking hand as he tried to write legibly. It read, "**I am overwhelmed with a sense of the goodness of God**." Allen Gardiner. (adapted from sermon central). Allen didn't LOSE to a broken body, he WON to a good God. He was called home after doing all he could for Jesus. Like Epaphroditus of old, he was sick from his call – and gave all he could.

At the same time, Saul was needed for the long haul, and had to learn to eat right, hydrate well, and rest when the time was given by God. He couldn't be DRIVEN by ministry, he needed to be DIRECTED by Jesus. Elijah learned that long before... A walk with God may need more prayer time, or it may be time to take a day and rest before God. We need to learn to pace ourselves in our ministries... These were some beginning lessons that helped flavor Saul's expectations and temper his steps... and they should ours as well.

Some of the initial lessons of faith are the hardest simply because they set the expectation for the rest of our time of service to the King.

Paul's Response to the Roman World:
"Getting Started: False Start"

"It is hard not to take off when there is so much at stake!" I could *SO* understand what the linebacker was saying in that locker room interview. Yet, the false starts cost penalties, and the penalties probably cost the team the game and the series. You can understand the problem. That man is lined up opposite some of the largest and most powerful men any of us will *ever* have the misfortune of opposing. Every player is hungry to *win*. No player wants to miss a "beat". Each wants to cover his man or his territory... but the quarterback's syncopated count can easily draw the overanxious into stepping forward on the line at the wrong time. **False starts happen all the time in the NFL.** Once a player jumps over the line of scrimmage before the ball is in play – a penalty ensues... because false starts incur penalties.

Unfortunately, they happen all the time in **LIFE** too... They happen when young people **rush to feel grown up** and engage in activities that are Biblically wrong and emotionally harmful for the stage of life they are in. The penalties for sinful engagement include mental tapes of memories that do not please God, along with a raft of other consequences. A false start happens when a **couple rushes into marriage** – and then finds the need for hours of counsel to unravel the mess they make in each other's lives to get back to the beginning of the marriage and make it work. There is a penalty for "false start" marriage. Since marriage is a covenant to remain together no matter what happens, Biblically sensitive people that unadvisedly rush into marriage should plan hours of counseling in their "Day Timers". False starts happen when **we make that major purchase and sign for the credit**, without carefully measuring the effect on our bank account and monthly expenses. The months and years that follow help us reflect on why that was a bad decision – but we are stuck in it. The penalties are numerous, but I suspect don't need much elaboration for many who are considering this lesson.

Our story today is not about someone who made a "false start" by doing something morally wrong. Rather, it is a warning about the need **to allow a time for education and transformation from the Spirit of God and the "marinating in the Word" that is necessary to be fully useful to the Lord**.

We have to admit that we are a culture that is much more about DOING than PREPARING. We seem to want to "get right into things"! At the same time, this isn't a new phenomenon. If there **was anyone that would have been *tempted* to push past the training stage**, it was the Apostle Paul. After all, he came to Messiah with substantial pedigree and accomplishments – even in the Word itself! Not only that, but his forceful personality and keen mind would have made listening to "lesser speakers" a difficult task at least, while allowing the misuse of Scripture in a class where he was sitting would be absolutely an intolerable circumstance. He was a man that was **given a mind and voice for God,** and wanted to **use** it... but God knew that **tempering and soaking in God's Word and Spirit** was essential. It is for that reason God "benched" Saul of Tarsus for a time, then led him through obscure ministry in small circles before He released Saul to the greater ministry of church planting and Apostleship ministry. This time included critical lessons learned in the heat of the desert, and the apparent insignificance of the more rural regions of Cilician and Syria before God opened to Paul his life's assignment. Those training years offered setbacks that helped Paul later in the ministry to recognize God's good hand despite tough times. Here was the big lesson...

Key Principle: God is in no hurry unfolding His outreach plan and His personnel assignments. He works at seasoning, training and molding carefully each servant He will use for important upcoming assignments. As a result, we must stop rushing God's

transformation and let His changes both *inform* and *infuse* us.

It can be incredibly hard for a zealous, young believer to have the patience to follow God and **not drag God along behind him or her**. God's plan is **GOD'S PLAN**... and He is under no obligation to match my *timing*, or my insightful understanding as to how things should play out. I must learn to **listen** to His voice, **follow** His lead, and **rest** in His arms when He blocks the way forward. Look at the place Saul of Tarsus learned these lessons. There are three passages that overlap. The first is from Dr. Luke's record in the Book of Acts:

*Acts 9:19b: "...Now for **several days he was with the disciples who were at Damascus**, 20 and **immediately he [began] to proclaim Jesus** in the **synagogues**, saying, "He is the Son of God." 21 All those hearing him continued to be amazed, and were saying, "Is this not he who in Jerusalem destroyed those who called on this name, and [who] had come here for the purpose of bringing them bound before the chief priests?"*

Before we look carefully at the passage, let's be clear – we are not talking about LAZINESS in the Kingdom. Saul wasn't set aside and drawn in slowly because he was reticent to jump in – quite the opposite. Saul was, like anyone who comes to Christ with a leadership personality, only too eager to move into the ministry without allowing time to have his mind transformed and renewed... and the church is often so eager to see this work that it may not easily recognize the need for curing, maturing and tempering...

Look at what happened when he first found Jesus and had his eyesight renewed! The Saul that condemned those who followed Jesus went right in to the Bema of the "Straight Street Synagogue" and began preaching the message of the Risen Christ (Acts 9:19-20)! People were not sure what to make of what he was saying (Acts 9:21). This record reminds us of some significant problems we create in "jumping the gun" on training:

Problem 1: When we move too quickly people are DISTRACTED by US – and may not be able to properly evaluate the message we bring.

There are some who believe that those who come to Jesus should immediately be put "on the line" to evangelize. They argue that these are people with the most direct contacts with the world – because they have just made a decision to come to Jesus. With a greater list of contacts, it is easier to engage lost men and women. The argument is repeatedly made: "We are called to make disciples of Jesus!" and off they run, pulling the uninformed and untransformed behind them. The zeal of the new convert makes the call for immediate action an appealing transition from the old life – but it is as dangerous as placing men on the front lines of a physical battle without a "boot camp" training experience.

Again, we are not arguing for laziness, and certainly one can – and should – share Christ with those around them as a natural part of "not denying Him before men" (cp. Mt. 10:33, though the context of that passage is not exactly and directly applicable in many cases). There is a need for holy boldness, and a call for spiritual sensitivity for the lost from the day of our new birth. At the same time, there is a need to for transformation of our minds and tempering of our spirit by God's Spirit – and that process is not instantaneous regardless of the knowledge we possess at salvation. Here is the truth:

We cannot make disciples until we learn how to become one.

We will not get people to truly follow Jesus until we learn to follow Jesus. For that reason, Paul later revealed that **God stepped in at the moment Saul was growing in strength** and sent him away. Compare Acts 9:19-21 with a later writing that offers another window to the lessons of the early days to the Galatians. In this passage, the Apostle is reflecting back on what happened in his early days with more specificity than Luke recorded in Acts:

*Galatians 1:13 For you have heard of my former manner of life in Judaism, how I used to persecute the church of God beyond measure and tried to destroy it; 14 and I was advancing in Judaism beyond many of my contemporaries among my countrymen, being more extremely zealous for my ancestral traditions. 15 But when God, who had set me apart [even] from my mother's womb and called me through His grace, was pleased 16 to reveal His Son in me so that I might preach Him among the Gentiles, **I did not immediately consult with flesh and blood**, 17 nor did I go up to Jerusalem to those who were apostles before me; but I went away to Arabia, and returned once more to Damascus.*

Even with all the training that preceded his coming to Christ, there was a need for the Saul of Tarsus to get alone with Jesus and learn to follow Him. The point of Galatians 1 was clearly to argue that Saul received his message from God, and not a consensus vote of any earthly group, but the fact is that God stepped in and sent him off when the Master could have used him mightily from day one.

Acts 9 is a truncated record of what took place in Saul's early ministry. The order of the events, if one looks carefully at Galatians 1, appears to be as follows:

1. Baptism by Ananias in Damascus (Acts 9:18).
2. Preaching right after his salvation in the synagogues of Damascus (Acts 9:19-21).

3. An extended time in Nabatea (probably in modern Jordan) for discipleship by the Savior (Gal. 1:13-17).
4. After training, another campaign in Damascus led to the plot to kill him – a long time after his salvation (Acts 9:22-25). Look at the record of Saul's return to Damascus in Acts 9:

*Acts 9:22 But **Saul kept increasing in strength** and **confounding the Jews who lived at Damascus** by proving that this [Jesus] is the Christ. 23 When many days had elapsed, the **Jews plotted together to do away with him**, 24 but their plot became known to Saul. They were also watching the gates day and night so that they might put him to death; 25 but his disciples took him by night and **let him down through [an opening in] the wall**, lowering him in a large **basket**.*

Luke signaled that 9:23 was LONG AFTER 9:19 and 20, but is is easy to miss in the narrative. It appears that since Saul could become the DISTRACTION, God's pattern was first to change him – and ground him with sufficient stability to preach the Gospel in the face of steady opposition. This highlights a second problem:

Problem 2: When we move too quickly we haven't grown strong and stable enough– and that will cause us to be too easily removed from the battle.

Consider the sufferings that were ahead for the Apostle Paul! Ask yourself, "What kind of training should Paul have had to be prepared for this list?"

*2 Cor. 11:23b "...Are they servants of Christ? -- I speak as if insane-- I more so; in far more **labors**, in far more **imprisonments**, **beaten** times without number, often in **danger** of death. 24 Five times I received from the Jews thirty-nine [lashes]. 25 Three times I was beaten with* *rods*, once I was **stoned**, three times I was **shipwrecked**, a night and a day I have spent in the deep. 26 [I have been] on frequent journeys, in **dangers from rivers**, dangers from **robbers**, dangers from [my] **countrymen**, dangers from the **Gentiles**, dangers in the **city**, dangers in the **wilderness**, dangers on the **sea**, dangers among **false brethren**; 27 [I have been] in labor and hardship, through many **sleepless nights**, in **hunger and thirst**, often **without food**, in **cold** and **exposure**. 28 Apart from [such] external things, there is the **daily pressure on me [of] concern for all the churches**. 29 Who is weak without my being weak? Who is led into sin without my intense concern?

Now let me ask you this" "Based on the way you see things going in our world, how strongly should we be training the next generation of believers?" Look at the list again in 2 Corinthians 11.

- Paul was trained to recognize the need to labor and not expect others to pay for God's call in his life.

- Paul was trained to believe that God was faithful even when he was unfairly imprisoned for his faith.

- Paul didn't think that knowing Jesus and the faithfulness of God was somehow breached when he was physically attacked – whether by "men" or by "nature".

- Paul didn't think that he was entitled in Christ to never be left hungry or thirsty – he saw God as meeting his needs even when his stomach growled and was empty.

- Paul recognized that ministry meant pressure, and that pressure wasn't a sign that he didn't trust God nor that God wasn't being good to him – it was hard to carry the burdens of leadership of men and women in their sinful state.

I stopped reading in 2 Corinthians before I got to the point that Paul was making in the passage... that he was TRAINED for what he was doing beforehand. Look again at 2 Corinthians 11, this time in the ending verses of the chapter...

2 Corinthians 11:30 If I have to boast, I will boast of what pertains to my weakness. 31 The God and Father of the Lord Jesus, He who is blessed forever, knows that I am not lying. 32 In Damascus the ethnarch under Aretas the king was guarding the city of the Damascenes in order to seize me, 33 and I was let down in a basket through a window in the wall, and [so] escaped his hands.

The apostle went back to the time, early in his ministry, when God first rescued him through the wall of Damascus. He had already learned that life wasn't going to be amenable to his message, and that ministry for Jesus was going to be a battle. He learned that civil authorities were already going to be used by the "Prince of the Air" to fight the Prince of All Heaven. He was rescued from Damascus, but read the play and saw the hand of God because of the three years of training in the Arabian desert.

Let me say it plainly: A Christian that is trained to think that "God is faithful" only when their belly is full, when their bankbook is fat and when their government is encouraging is not ready for troubled times – but will be cut down quickly by a vicious and mighty fallen prince and his followers. Our spiritual training must change to that of the early church – to anticipate hatred and match it with love; to anticipate unfair treatment and match it with fervent and unending prayer; to anticipate physical weakness and need and match it with trust that God has not left us without the rich resources found in Him alone.

Our training must widen the eyes of disciples to recognize the historic reality that darkness has often seemed to be stronger than light – but that God will emerge victorious in the end just as He has promised. We dare not become impatient in trouble and allow circumstances alter our view of God's goodness and faithfulness. Yet, these truths come from **tempering and training** – and will require (in many cases) a reversal of modern trends of discipleship instruction.

Paul didn't just "learn it from Jesus" and then know everything. He needed to learn from other me and "fit into" the church structure if his ministry was going to be supported and successful for the Master. The END of his training came with his beheading – not earlier! Let's continue with the story of Saul's early training with two passages that tell us what happened:

*Acts 9:26 When **he came to Jerusalem**, he was trying to associate with the disciples; but **they were all afraid of him**, not believing that he was a disciple. 27 But **Barnabas took hold of him and brought him to the apostles** and described to them how he had seen the Lord on the road, and that He had talked to him, and how at Damascus **he had spoken out boldly in the name of Jesus**. 28 And he was with them, moving about freely in **Jerusalem, speaking out boldly** in the name of the Lord. 29 And he was talking and **arguing with the Hellenistic [Jews]**; but they were attempting to put him to **death**. 30 But when the brethren learned [of it], they **brought him down to Caesarea and sent him away to Tarsus**. 31 So the church throughout all Judea and Galilee and Samaria enjoyed peace, being built up; and going on in the fear of the Lord and in the comfort of the Holy Spirit, it continued to increase.*

*Galatians 1:18 Then **three years later** I went up to **Jerusalem** to become acquainted with **Cephas**, and stayed with him **fifteen days**. 19 But I did not see any other of the apostles except **James**, the Lord's brother. 20 (Now in what I am writing to you, I assure you before God that I am not lying.) 21 **Then I went into the regions of Syria and Cilicia**. 22 I was **[still] unknown by sight to the churches of Judea** which were in*

Christ; 23 but only, they kept hearing, "He who once persecuted us is now preaching the faith which he once tried to destroy." 24 And they were glorifying God because of me.

The three events that are referenced in Acts 9, Galatians 1 and in Acts 22 should be woven together in our minds:

- Paul's trip to Jerusalem **three years after his conversion** (Galatians 1:18) – where he stayed with Peter for **fifteen days** (Galatians 1:17-18) – but **saw only James and Peter** was the setting of a vision setting out his Gentile ministry (Acts 22:15-21).

- When the plot to stop Paul's disputations among Hellenistic Jews was uncovered at Jerusalem in that half-month, **Paul was escorted to Caesarea and sent back to Tarsus** (Acts 9:29-30). Some scholars believe the first of his shipwrecks may have occurred along the way home from Caesarea (2 Cor. 11:25).

- Paul preached from his home base in Tarsus, occasionally traveling to surrounding Syrian and Cilician territories (Galatians 1:21-24). He **stayed there four or five years**, when Barnabas sought him in Tarsus and brought him to Antioch (Acts 11:25-26).

That means that although Paul came to Jesus in the year 36 CE – he wasn't used by God as a missionary until at least **SEVEN YEARS LATER**.

Note: 2 Cor. 11:32 reminds that Paul escaped Damascus shortly after his salvation, while Aretas was king of Arabia (which took place between 36-39 CE). Eusebius recorded that Paul came to Messiah at the beginning of Aretas' reign. The three years in Damascus and Nabatean territory would have taken place, by this reckoning, between 36-39 CE. The remaining years (39-44

CE) were likely consumed with Paul's Tarsian and Cilician excursions until he was brought to Antioch.

Problem 3: When we move too quickly in our training we learn how to mimic other men – but not hear Jesus' voice.

In the passages of Acts 9 and Galatians 1 we skipped an insightful few verses that explain Paul's redirection by Jesus. For that we have to go to Acts 22. The text was one of Paul's defenses after his arrest, and the detail he included fits exactly into the time we are looking at from his life history…

Acts 22:17 "It happened when I returned to Jerusalem and was praying in the temple, that I fell into a trance, 18 and I saw Him saying to me, 'Make haste, and get out of Jerusalem quickly, because they will not accept your testimony about Me.' 19 "And I said, 'Lord, they themselves understand that in one synagogue after another I used to imprison and beat those who believed in You. 20 And when the blood of Your witness Stephen was being shed, I also was standing by approving, and watching out for the coats of those who were slaying him.' 21 "And He said to me, 'Go! For I will send you far away to the Gentiles.'"

Here is the point: Paul was SO ready in the eyes of MEN to reach out to other Jews. He was a trained Pharisee. He had both the education, and the ability to lean into the Jerusalem synagogues and be heard. His voice would have been welcome in Jewish evangelism. No apostle could have been expected to do a better job in those tough rooms… yet that was not his calling. Jesus made clear that he was being sent to pig eating pagans.

Notice that Paul OBJECTED in the passage. He was a KNOWN QUANTITY to the Jewish leadership. His transformation would have been easiest to map in front of those who knew him in his "before Jesus" days (Acts 22:19-20). Yet, Jesus commanded redirection. He commanded him AWAY from Jerusalem, and away from Jewish ministry. Paul was able to recognize the voice of Jesus, even if he couldn't yet recognize the wisdom of God's direction. That is what tempering does. That is what training yields. That is what transformation creates – ears to hear the Spirit's call through the Word of God. A renewed mind is a mind that can hear from the Word of God and spiritually discern direction – in spite of the way it looks in the physical setting... but that takes time to learn.

Have you noticed that God's early training of Paul wasn't EASY? His training included some small successes (some people heard the Gospel and were unable to refute Paul's testimony), but it also included things like death threats and hot retreats into the desert among strangers...Why didn't God make it EASY for Paul? Because God is into preparation, not comfort. When everything is EASY, our growth is little. When it is hard, we learn to stand up.

Do you know how a giraffe is born? The average gestation period for giraffe is approximately **15 months** (453-464 days). Giraffe gives birth at a 'calving ground' - mothers have been known to return to where they were born to have their own babies. In herds, calving is often synchronized to provide safety in numbers against predators. Yet, the process of having the calf seems very hard indeed! When the baby giraffe starts its journey down the birth canal, the mother seeks out a spot where there are no bushes, just flat open ground. The "momma giraffe" gives birth **standing up**, requiring the newborn to fall about **two meters** to the ground! Designed for such an abrupt entry into the world, a newborn calf can stand up and run within an hour of being born. When the calf hits the ground, it may not move of its own accord. If it rolls over and just lies there with legs all curled up under it, the momma may take her very strong legs and kick the calf, causing to fly across the dirt. If the calf does not stand up, the mother may go over and kick it again, until the calf finally stands up. She knows that the calf needs to learn, and her offspring must remember how to stand so it can save itself later in a time of danger.

Let me ask you to do something this week. "Stop asking God to end the swift kicking. Start asking Him what He has been trying to get you to learn!" And don't forget... it will take time to soak in His Word and follow His voice... but you have His Spirit.

Look at the bright side: **God didn't make you a giraffe!**

Remember, God is in no hurry unfolding His outreach plan and His personnel assignments. He works at seasoning, training and sculpting carefully each servant He will use for important upcoming assignments. We need to soak it in, and then allow the world to get it when it is squeezed out of us!

Paul's Response to the Roman World:
"Paul Joins a Team: Making Connection"

It was fifty-two years ago this summer that President John F. Kennedy announced the launch of the **Telstar Communications Satellite** that connected in near "real time" the European continent to the USA by way of microwave signal. This was the first "instant wireless signal", that allowed for both dynamic two-way communication and live picture broadcast. That first television broadcast was, in fact, the press conference that "linked" the western world together, and bridged the ocean without the physical constraints of tethering wires. In a real way, this was the beginning of wireless connection that has connected much of the world together without wires. You may be interested to know that there are now just over **7 billion people on the planet**, and **6.8 billion cell phones**. It is true, not every area of our globe is covered, and some people have multiple phones, but I doubt President Kennedy could have envisioned that a single satellite would begin connections that would put whole computers in purses and pockets of people around the globe in the form of cell phones... We live in the connected world, and most of us don't even think about it.

I find it interesting watching how different personalities handle this constant connection. For instance, I cannot tell you how often I am in professional settings where the other party I am meeting seems to believe that a "text message" always trumps live meeting. During a given meeting, they will constantly check the "ding" on their phone, as if the survival of the population of small, third world countries depends on having real-time access to them every moment of the day. I find it distracting, and, yes... a bit rude. I took the time to make an appointment, and it seems that I should have simply texted them – and I would have gotten immediate attention to my query. Ah, these are but a few of the problems of constant connection! Yet, **connection is essential**

to all of us these days. Consider how different life was before easy and constant connection!

Hold that thought about connection, because it is extremely relevant to our lesson from the Word... For a few moments, I want us to take another step together in our studies on the "Life and Ministry of Saul of Tarsus", better known to believers as the Apostle Paul – and look at how the important lesson of connection was forged in his life...

We met Saul at the stoning of Stephen recorded in Acts 7, and took a quick overview of his life and ministry – just to get our "feet wet" in the details of his life. In the second study, we watched as Jesus broke the proud stride of the "Pharisee on a mission" and cast him to the ground in a blinding light. He met Jesus there, and Jesus took away his physical sight for three days, to give him spiritual insight that would change his eternity. Though well-educated and erudite before meeting the Savior in a vision, we noted that Saul wasn't ready until he relearned the basics of life, and then had intense training for an extended period under the work of the Spirit's transformation and Jesus' discipleship in the desert. We watched Saul take his "first steps" in his new faith – and then celebrated the work of God in him over seven years of reshaping.

In this lesson, we want to bridge the gap between his time of early learning and his first mission journey, by looking at the Scripture for the next move of God in his life. Let's summarize where we are this way:

- First, we can observe the thirty plus years of life of a Pharisee who loved the Law – but didn't have a personal relationship with God.

- Second, the Word offered an excellent picture of the meeting place between the Savior and the would-be servant.

- Third, the early training and reshaping took place in initial success in Damascus and a hiatus in the desert to learn from the Savior, followed by an attempt on his life. Escaping Damascus, he met some key leaders of the faith but got a vision to from God to leave Jewish ministry and head for the diaspora – back to Tarsus. The temptation to "jump ahead of God's call" was overcome, and Saul got busy ministering in small places, and learned faithfulness long after the newness wore off.

- Now we see the one lacking piece that will make or break the rest of his ministry – the careful making of **connection** to the other believers in the body of Christ (the church). With this, we see an important principle…

Key Principle: The believer was not called to follow Jesus alone, but to work in vital connection to the body of Christ.

The Apostle Paul carried the weight of the believers of his day – there is no doubt about it. He felt it when they turned on one another, hurt one another, or acted sinfully and brought derision on the name of the Savior. He constantly urged the believers to see themselves as connected together – all ONE in Christ. In one discussion, as Paul was writing about spiritual gifts – those special enabling powers given by God at the time of our salvation – he told the believers at Corinth that they were joined together… they were part of one another. He wrote:

1 Corinthians 12:12 For even as the body is one and [yet] has many members, and all the members of the body, though they are many, are one body, so also is Christ. 13 For by one Spirit we were all baptized into one body, whether Jews or Greeks, whether slaves or free, and we were all made to drink of one Spirit. 14 For the body is not one member, but many. 15 If the foot says, "Because I am not a hand, I am not [a part] of the body," it is not for this reason any the less [a part] of the body. ... 18 But now God has placed the members, each one of them, in the body, just as He desired. ... 20 But now there are many members, but one body. 21 And the eye cannot say to the hand, "I have no need of you"; or again the head to the feet, "I have no need of you." ... 24 ... But God has [so] composed the body, giving more abundant honor to that [member] which lacked, 25 so that there may be no division in the body, but [that] the members may have the same care for one another. 26 And if one member suffers, all the members suffer with it; if [one] member is honored, all the members rejoice with it. 27 Now you are Christ's body, and individually members of it.

When we read that passage, there are five things that become very clear:

- First, any differences between believers (in terms of their exercise of gifts) must not suggest a different body connection, only a different function within the body. We are all pulling together in Christ – even if we are doing it differently than our best Christian friend.

- Second, our backgrounds aren't supposed to be a dividing factor. Our race, our past and our status in society are melted away as we join with one another.

- Third, every role in the body is important – though not all are as "visible" to the whole.

- Fourth, individuals may find a cause to rejoice or cry – and we are to be able to it together. We are joined to each other in grief, sorrow, joy and celebration!

- Fifth, connection is the key to healthy activity. A body that loses a part loses health and wholeness. In the same way, we are to grow into our need of one another – caring about the absenting of one from the others.

Here is my question: "How did Paul come to that conclusion?" I know, you and I recognize the words were not merely Paul's own – but he was moved by God's Spirit to write what he did. At the same time, he agreed with the words. How did he grow from the rugged individualist leader type to one who was so very connected to others? I suspect God taught him through the incredible benefits of connection. In the early stages of his ministry, just as he was learning to be faithful in the small assignments, God was sculpting Paul. **He was learning the value of connection.**

Five Advantages of Connection:

I have been finishing the work on my upstairs bathroom, and have been putting the cabinetry on the walls, and finishing the wiring of the bathroom. To help me get the look Dottie wanted, we went to IKEA. Someone has quipped that IKEA is Swedish for "puzzle maker" – and if you have ever bought their products you know why that is both funny and painful. I admit it – I love their cabinets and rooms, but have never seen so many parts simply to hang a door! In the thousands of little pieces they give you as part of the pack, I have only one warning… be careful to keep everything together and organized. You will need every little Swedish "do-dad" they give you to put their furnishings together! Those little connectors are essential!

While we are thinking about those little connectors, let's think about the "body connectors" that we have for the body of Christ. We get together in tons of little meetings. Many of them are not very important on the face of them – but people who pray and play together learn to stay together. When you know people well, it is harder to begin to believe bad things shared with you about them. You KNOW them… and that happened because of countless meals together, meetings, little tasks – time spent together! There are INCREDIBLE ADVANTAGES TO CONNECTION. I want to mention five of them that Paul learned at this stage of his walk – just before God called him into mission service along dusty roads, on wind-whipped ships, and surrounded by the smell of cooking pig meat.

Connection offers protection
(Acts 9:29-30)

First, connection offers protection when the enemy attacks – and he WILL attack. Look in Acts 9:29-30:

9:29 And he was talking and arguing with the Hellenistic [Jews]; but they were attempting to put him to death. 30 But when the brethren learned [of it], they brought him down to Caesarea and sent him away to Tarsus.

In our last lesson we breezed by the death threat against Paul. It was an important lesson to the young Christian – that walking with God was not going to be without it enemies and hazards. In fact, when you gave your life to Christ, the enemy of Jesus became YOUR enemy as well. As an unbeliever, Satan had no reason to get too far into your life. Most of the damage in terms of sin came from the influence of the world (where Satan has a hand) and the works of the flesh (which are bent toward evil since the Fall of man). Yet, when you surrendered your life to Jesus to follow Him and trust Him – you got a target on your back. If you move forward with your witness – you should expect the wicked one to pay attention to you in a whole new way!

Though other believers cannot put on all the spiritual armor God called the believer to wear – your brothers and sisters in Christ DO have a role to play when you are under attack. Do you remember where Paul wrote about the connection that offers protection? Ephesians 6 reminded the believers at Ephesus of the common Roman armor they saw everyday as soldiers passed through the city. Paul took inventory and assessed the implements for a fight – then applied those pieces of armor to the spiritual war. He urged the believers of Ephesus to be strengthened in God's power (10). How?

- By using the resources God gave them (Eph. 6:11);
- By **identifying the real enemy** (Eph. 6:11b-12);
- By **deliberately putting on all the protection provided by God** (Eph. 6:13).

Paul wrote of two types of armor.

The **FIRST TYPE** was that armor which must **always** be at the **ready**. If there was a lull in the battle, the fighter was **not** to remove the **first three implements**. He indicated that in the verb form "always having" the:

a. Belt of truthfulness: (alethia: truth as content) vulnerable area, carefully protected (14); Paul was not addressing the truth of salvation (as in v. 17 and the sword, Word), but rather the **commitment to truthfulness** of the believer!

b. Breastplate of righteousness (holy choices): covering heart, able to take direct blows when positioned correctly (14b), breaks your heart when not maintained. In the Hebrew world, the "heart" is the mind! (Prov. 23:7; Mark 7:21). Paul does not refer to self-righteousness (Eph. 2:8-9), nor of imputed righteousness (2 Cor. 5:21), but of a **life practice of righteousness**, or holy living.

c. Sandal guard straps fixed in position to provide a firm stand with the Gospel: metal tabs that protected the surface of the foot with cleats to hold the soldier in place. Paul refers to the **unmovable faith in the Gospel** to bring peace in the life of the lost.

The **SECOND TYPE** of armor was indicated in the poor translation of "Above all" (v.16). The grammar was NOT indicating the shield is more important, but is linked to the verb form of all of the next three items. They were to appropriate at the time necessary the:

d. Blocking shield of faith (theuron; large shield to block arrows; 4.5 feet by 2.5 feet., cp. Psalm 18:30). His reference is not to "belief" as such, but to "trust" that changes our view of ourselves and the world around us. When the battle rages, use the shield. 1) they were effective when **locked together**; 2) they were effective when **held tightly and trusted** and all remained in place.

e. Helmet of salvation (refers to the **protection of the transformed mind**) when we understand that our salvation has a PAST aspect: justification; a PRESENT aspect: sanctification; and a FUTURE aspect, our eventual glorification. We must see things through God's eyes and learn to call the battle by His Word!

f. Sword of the Spirit: the WORD (RAMA: From the word "to pour, an utterance") of God. The "machaira" dagger is not the broad sword, rhomphaia). A **specific Word from God** that He gives to take a **direct shot at the enemy**!

It is the blocking shield that reminds us of the protection from connection. Only a wall of shields would block, intimidate and cause advance. Alone, the soldier was just a guy with a leather covered device. Together, the wall of soldiers was ghastly if they were advancing on your line!

Let's be clear: **the enemy always looks for the believer that thinks they can stand alone**. Without accountability, without engagement of others, without placing ourselves deliberately under the spiritual authority of godly men – we are like the wandering wildebeest on the prairie – we look much like "supper" to a hungry lion.

Connection offers inspection
(Acts 11:19-24)

Deliberate connection to the body also offers something else – it offers the opportunity to have our life inspected by another. That isn't the negative that some may hear. Listen to the passage that helped shape the early church's sense of inspection:

*Acts 11:19 So then those who were scattered because of the persecution that occurred in connection with Stephen made their way to Phoenicia and Cyprus and Antioch, speaking the word to **no one except to Jews alone**. 20 But there were some of them, men of Cyprus and Cyrene, who came to Antioch and [began] **speaking to the Greeks** also, preaching the Lord Jesus. 21 And the hand of the Lord was with them, and a large number who believed turned to the Lord. 22 The news about them reached the ears of the church at Jerusalem, and **they sent Barnabas off to Antioch**. 23 Then when he arrived and **witnessed the grace of God**, he **rejoiced** and [began] to **encourage** them all with resolute heart to **remain [true] to the Lord**; 24 for he was a good man, and full of the Holy Spirit and of faith. And **considerable numbers were brought to the Lord**.*

God was doing something in Antioch that wasn't happening in Jerusalem. In fact, Jerusalem had no desire for it to happen. God was opening the door to the Gentile world – a blessing that became the most disturbing problem to the early church of the first century. Many of the epistles, letters written from church leaders to local churches and other leaders, addressed that very issue.

The text related that most believers were sharing the message of Jesus WITHIN Judaism, even after they began to scatter with rising persecution (Acts 11:19). A few began to speak to Greeks – whether they were proselytes to Judaism or not we do not know – but they clearly went outside the normal frame of practiced ministry. Remember, the whole "church thing" was still new. Remember also that Jesus promised the Apostles they would be called upon to "bind" (forbid) and "loose" (allow) things as they sought the Spirit's direction (Matthew 18:18).

When believers heard about the ministry to the Gentiles, they dispatched a godly and encouraging man to look carefully into the matter. What he found shocked, and then delighted him. God was doing something no one foresaw! He encouraged them to continue, and many came to Christ (Acts 11:23-24). The connection between the groups made inspection possible, and allowed the believers to share even greater joy – instead of one group hiding what they were doing from another out of fear. Why? **Connection tears down fear**. It bridges differences. It allows us to explain ourselves to a caring ear, so that we are challenged if wrong, and strengthened if correct. The group felt affirmed, understood and even more interconnected as a result of Barnie's visit!

Connection offers endorsement
(Acts 11:25-26)

Paul probably heard about what happened in Antioch later, but he also personally experienced it a short time after the first Greeks were coming to Jesus. Follow the story as Dr. Luke offered it...

*Acts 11:25 And he left for Tarsus **to look for Saul;** 26 and when he had found him, he **brought him to Antioch**. And for an entire **year** they **met with the church** and **taught** considerable numbers; and the **disciples were first called Christians** in Antioch.*

What incredible verses! Saul was about seven years old in Messiah, and he was faithfully serving God while making tents. He was part of the fellowship of churches – teaching and sharing

–but he was "nobody particularly important" at that time. It was the connection that Barnabas made to him that changed all that. Barnie knew what Saul had to offer. He recognized the need for a critical thinker, as well as a careful learner of the Word. Barnie was convinced that God was at work, but he knew that his evaluation needed to be examined in light of the Word of God. Who better than that tough minded Pharisee from Tarsus? Saul followed because Saul felt connected. They met for a year with believers in Antioch because they knew they were connected to one Savior, fighting one battle, working for one cause.

Did you note the outcome? Of course there were some great Bible studies, and yes... there were no doubt more added to the Lord... but look at the end of what we read...Christians got their name! They first LOOKED LIKE a body of Christ – sounding like the Savior and acting in that familiar loving yet decisive way. They got called "Christians" because they acted like "little Christs" – followers in DEED. **Connection offered the opportunity for Saul to be endorsed** by Barnabas, and it offered the opportunity for the whole body to be commended as walking like Jesus!

Connection offers context
(2 Corinthians 12:2-7)

It would be easy to skip an important event that appears to have happened right at this time. About fourteen years after the events of Acts 11, Paul was writing to the church at Corinth, and he mentioned an event that probably fit the time we are studying – so it is worth mentioning. Saul was not ONLY learning how to walk with Jesus and serve Him from other leaders, he was learning from the Master Himself. Once again, a vision assisted Saul's growth – and it will help us to see how God used connection to set the vision in a context of ministry to people. First, the record:

2 Corinthians 12:2 I know a man in Christ who fourteen years ago-- whether in the body I do not know, or out of the body I do not know, God knows-- such a man was caught up to the third heaven. 3 And I know how such a man-- whether in the body or apart from the body I do not know, God knows—4 was caught up into Paradise and heard inexpressible words, which a man is not permitted to speak. 5 On behalf of such a man I will boast; but on my own behalf I will not boast, except in regard to [my] weaknesses. 6 For if I do wish to boast I will not be foolish, for I will be speaking the truth; but I refrain [from] [this], so that no one will credit me with more than he sees [in] me or hears from me. 7 Because of the surpassing greatness of the revelations, for this reason, to keep me from exalting myself, there was given me a thorn in the flesh, a messenger of Satan to torment me-- to keep me from exalting myself!

Paul was in the midst of a letter that offered three basic statements. 2 Corinthians offered an explanation in chapters 1-7 as to why Paul told the church at Corinth he was coming, but then did not show up. In chapter 8-9, Paul renewed his expectation that the people of Corinth would complete the collection for the believers at Jerusalem. In the end of the letter, Paul exhorted the believers of Corinth to follow proper leadership and behave well (2 Cor. 10-13). While the letter had a somewhat defensive tone in places, it was clear that some believers in Corinth were "bad mouthing" the Apostle in his absence. Some thought they were "just as qualified" to offer God's direction as Paul – and they said so! They were arrogant in his absence, and his connection to them would help them get back in line.

The passage we read was about Paul's own opportunity to visit Heaven in a vision. God used that, as he did long before with Ezekiel, to secure Paul through difficult days. His glimpse at the majesty of our God bolstered him through troubled times. Yet it was very personal. The things he saw were not to be shared – they were for him alone.

Did he get a "big head" and walk arrogantly because of the vision – not really. He got along with God's deep and abiding encouragement something else. He got a "thorn in the flesh". He got a weakness. God didn't just want to him to be strong and privileged – but dependent and weak. The GREAT APOSTLE PAUL would need others to do the late night writing and correspondence – because his eyes evidently were not always working. Connection offers us a way to be real, to place all our blessing in a context of real life – and to walk with others as ONE OF THEM. **Paul was connected to Christ by his incredible spiritual vision – and connected more deeply to other believers because of his faulty physical vision**. Paul could set his blessings in the context of his needs, and be a balanced and loving follower of Jesus.

Connection offers expanded vision (Acts 11:27-30; 12:25-13:3)

Just as Barnabas found that God was expanding the vision of ministry, so Paul learned that in the body were some attuned to needs he would not have sensed. Luke offered:

*Acts 11:27 Now at this time some prophets came down from Jerusalem to Antioch. 28 One of them named Agabus stood up and [began] to indicate by the Spirit that there would certainly be a **great famine all over the world**. And this took place in the [reign] of Claudius. 29 And in the proportion that any of the disciples had means, each of them determined to send [a contribution] for the **relief of the brethren living in Judea**. 30 And this they did, **sending it in charge of Barnabas and Saul** to the elders.*

Then later Luke offered:

Acts 12:25 And Barnabas and Saul returned from Jerusalem when they had fulfilled their mission, taking *along with [them] John, who was also called Mark. Acts 13:1 Now there were at Antioch, in the church that was [there], prophets and teachers: Barnabas, and Simeon who was called Niger, and Lucius of Cyrene, and Manaen who had been brought up with Herod the tetrarch, and Saul. 2 While they were ministering to the Lord and fasting, the Holy Spirit said, "**Set apart for Me Barnabas and Saul** for the work to which I have called them." 3 Then, when they had fasted and prayed and laid their hands on them, they sent them away.*

Look at both of these scenes and you cannot help but notice that God worked through the body of Messiah – as one part of the body was called on to assist the other part. Agabus made the room aware that trouble was coming. Others devised a plan to assist the fledgling church at Jerusalem and the Judean villages. Together they could tackle what no one could do alone. Together they could see what they could not see alone. Later, after Barnabas and Saul returned to Antioch, it was in the prayer meeting of the body that God set aside Barnabas and Saul for the work they were to do for Him. It was from their knees that God spoke to the ROOM, so that no one could later claim the men were self-appointed. A prayer meeting of the body yielded the first piercing into the darkness of the Roman world beyond the "drift" of the Gospel.

James Montgomery Boice told a story back in the days he pastored in Philadelphia. He spoke of **Lawrence of Arabia visiting Paris after World War I with some Arab friends**. He showed them around Paris, but what **fascinated them most was the faucet in their hotel room**. They spent hours turning it on and off; they thought it was wonderful. All they had to do was turn the handle, and they could get all the water they wanted. When time came to leave, Lawrence found them in the bathroom trying to detach the faucet. They explained, "It is very dry in Arabia. What we need are faucets. If we have them, we will have all the water we want." Lawrence had to explain that the effectiveness of the faucets lay in their connection to the pipeline.

I am living in a time when believers don't seem to realize that our power is not only from connection to the Spirit and to the Word – but also to each other. We were called to live, to walk and to serve in the context of community. The body of Christ has far too many parts that are proudly disconnecting themselves – and they are losing strength in the process. When the Spirit sent Barnabas and Saul out, it was not in disconnection – but in extension.

I want you to think for a moment about some men traveling in a river on a small raft. They didn't realize until too late they were close to waterfalls and rapids, and the small raft was being tugged more and more swiftly by the sweeping current into the rocks of the rapids. The men began to panic. Knocked from the raft, one man after another struggled as they were pulled toward the falls, and toward a certain death. One man spotted a tree limb growing from the shore and glanced off a rock in the direction of the shore, grabbing the limb and working his way slowly toward the shore. The limb was small and weak, but with patience and struggle – that man was safe on shore. In the meantime, another man saw a large log – it looked strong and stable. He grabbed the log as it moved by, and that choice led him to the falls and to his death. Though the log looked stronger, it was unattached to the shore. It was unconnected. It didn't lead to safety or strength. It led to death.

Believers must learn to connect and work at connection. That connection provides protection, inspection, endorsement, context and expanding vision. **The believer was not called to follow Jesus alone, but to work in vital connection to the body of Christ.**

Paul's Response to the Roman World:
"First Mission Journey: What do you expect?"

For any thoughtful young woman, expecting their first baby can be very exciting, but also a little scary. How do I know that is true? Well, for one thing, **I am a dad**. But even if I weren't, all I would have to know is that "<u>What to Expect When You're Expecting</u>" is a perennial New York Times bestseller and was rated by "USA Today" as one of the twenty-five most "influential books of the past quarter century". Some authorities report that more than 90% of pregnant American women have picked up this book for a look, with over 14.5 million copies in print in its *four* editions. It has spun off a website and a whole genre of other works in the subject area. Obviously, **the author struck a nerve** with child bearing women, and that nerve was **apprehension** and **uncertain expectation**.

What we expect from an experience has much to do with how we pass through that experience. I mention the book because the author obviously felt that **explaining the birthing process** and offering insights and testimony from those who have passed through the process would be incredibly helpful to one who is facing the experience. What is true in the process of birthing a child is also true in the process of birthing a church and a Gospel movement in a pagan world. The book of Acts offers the **"What to Expect When You're Expecting New Births in the Kingdom"** – and has been a bestseller for centuries! The book includes a record of "men on a mission from God" to reach into a pagan world, armed with God's Spirit and power, effectively fighting against God's adversary, the Devil. It isn't just a "nuts and bolts" look at outreach and church planting; it is a very personal, sometimes remarkably painful reflection of frail men on an exalted mission. It isn't the *men* you should be impressed with – but the gains God makes through, and always in spite of, these men as the Gospel powerfully changed lives.

If we are to see paganism again pressed by the power of God – we must know what we are "up against" in the spiritual world. We must know what to anticipate and how to prepare. We must be ready as individual believers for Satan's counterattack to the Gospel in our personal lives (where temptation can derail us), in the privacy of our own homes (where interpersonal strife can easily develop), in the ministry of our churches (where a group of natural hypocrites must come together and be transformed by renewing of our minds and hearts) and in our communities (where the Gospel is generally ignored, except when it is attacked). I am convinced that is why God gave to us the Book of Acts.

Key Principle: God's Word can help us reset expectations so that we can navigate life thoughtfully and positively as individuals and as a Gospel movement.

In this lesson we move from the early steps and preparations of the Apostle Paul to his first team ministry outreach - sent by the Spirit of God to unbelieving people who did not yet have any local church witness. That was the essence of Barnabas and Paul's job – to establish the church in new places by preaching the Gospel. They were to arrive, get an audience with local people (which began in the local synagogue of each town) and present the truth that Jesus **replaced the atonement system** of the Hebrew Scriptures – the killing of animals in sacrifices and the need to continually maintain one's right standing before God by regular participation in the sacrificial ceremonies. God had done a *new thing* that was **GOOD NEWS**, called "the Gospel". The message of the Gospel was that a full, complete and everlasting **JUSTIFICATION** (a permanent declaration of full payment for sin) before God could now be obtained by the surrender of one's heart and life to Jesus Christ. Because Jesus Himself bore the payment for all of our sins, Jesus could cancel the debt anyone had with God. As a perfect sacrifice, Jesus offered a "one size fits all" payment that need not be repeated in any further installments, nor amended in any way.

The Good News was, and still IS this: When a man, woman or child recognizes they are in need of a relationship with a Holy God, but are not righteous in and of themselves, they are able to ask Jesus to take His perfect payment (made in His own blood) to wash away their sin. All the remains of the breach between God and their heart is erased, and God willingly dwells within the life surrendered. When one asks for this, Jesus has promised in the Bible He would apply the payment and cancel their "rebellion caused" debt – and God acknowledged His agreement with His Son's sacrifice by raising Jesus from the dead. That was the essence of the Good News, and is the same Gospel that true followers of Jesus offer to a lost world today. It isn't a "get out of jail free" card – because the Gospel is costly – but not to the sinner. The good news of the Gospel is that I cannot pay, but Jesus already DID PAY.

The Prayer Room Pre-launch

Go back in the room where the first declared and intention outreach mission began in the first century. The record of what happened should help us set our expectations as people who follow God. I warn you, the record isn't what some are saying. It isn't the story of how people came to Jesus and everything got easy... not at all. Let's look at the beginning of Acts 13...

Acts 13:1 Now there were at Antioch, in the church that was [there], prophets and teachers: Barnabas, and Simeon who was called Niger, and Lucius of Cyrene, and Manaen who had been brought up with Herod the tetrarch, and Saul. 2 While they were ministering to the Lord and fasting, the Holy Spirit said, "Set apart for Me Barnabas and Saul for the work to which I have called them." 3 Then, when they had fasted and prayed and laid their hands on them, they sent them away. 4 So, being sent out by the Holy Spirit, they went down to Seleucia and from there they sailed to Cyprus.

The mission started with the leadership of a local church body in a prayer meeting. These were <u>mature</u> men. They were dedicated, reputable followers of Jesus that knew the source of spiritual power – from God's throne. Look at the names of the other men kneeling beside Paul:

- Barnabas was a Levitical Jew from Cyprus (Acts 4:36) who was actually named Joseph, but was more known as "Mr. Encouragement" than his family name!

- Simeon (Shim'on) was a Jew who was likely a black man from North African descent, and may have been the Cyrenian who carried the Cross of Jesus (though this is not certain). What we can assume is that he was a traveler in the Empire, and used his Latin name "Niger".

- Lucius of Cyrene may have been another black man, but many Cyrenians were transplants from the Italic peninsula, so we aren't sure.

- Manaen is a man we believe we know more about. The text reminds us that he was "brought up with Herod the Tetrarch (called Herod Antipas in the Gospels). He appears to have been raised by the mother of Archelaus and Antipas, both of whom were schooled in Rome as children. By the time of this prayer meeting, both "princes" were in exile to the Rhone region, banished from their former post. If Manaen were here, he'd be able to tell us some very interesting things about the Herodian dynasty. The fact is, though, he was a man of background and means, and now he was following Christ.

These were **men of prayer**. I cannot say it loud and long enough... no church and no Christian will ever become effective in the battle without prayer. It isn't a distraction and it isn't a luxury. When troubles come, prayer meetings fill... but in times we perceive "success" we become lax about the spiritual wrestling that happens from the knees.

These were also **men of service**. They didn't just "come to church to get something out of it" – they came, that day, to "minister to the Lord". They fasted and fixed their gaze on Heaven. There were no forms and programs – there was prayer and fasting. The forms may now be necessary, and the programs may attract the less fervent – but none of it replaces the prayer of godly people.

These were **obedient men**. They heard from God, and they followed God's Word. When God told them who to send and where, they fasted more, prayed more (in case God had more to add), and after some time they publicly placed on Barnabas and Saul (Paul) the responsibility and public symbol of a call to a specific ministry.

Let's stop for a moment and ask what we can learn from their experience. Could it be that our expectation for ministry ought to be like their experience? When serious believers seek God in fixed times of prayer and fasting might we be assured that God would direct the movement forward? Can we expect that God will move because we ASK Him to direct? Did not Jesus tell His disciples in the "Sermon on the Mount" (Matthew 5-7) that their Father knew what they needed and would not give them something else when they took the time to ask Him? Let's say it directly...

Expectation One: We should expect to need direction and supply from God. We will not always know what to do next in life or ministry – but God gave us prayer and our solution.

Salamis Proclamation

Acts 13:5 When they reached Salamis, they [began] to proclaim the word of God in the synagogues of the Jews; and they also had John as their helper.

Barnabas and Saul left Antioch and walked the fifteen miles to board a ship docked in nearby Seleucia that was bound for Barnabas' native island – Cyprus. They sailed about 100 miles, and harbored in at Salamis. For their time in that city, Luke (the author) offers only one verse – but it is not unimportant to our understanding. Look closely, and we can see three important details:

- When they arrived, the script they followed was the Word of God.

- They began in the synagogue, because that is where people with a background in atonement would be gathered, and the Gospel would make more sense in that audience. They didn't start at the pagan end of town – but at the place where people had some comprehension of the God of Abraham and His Word.

- They went as a team, but they added a younger helper. We have no information that leads us to conclude that God told them to seek out John Mark, but when they got to Cyprus, they added him to their team (probably at the behest of his uncle Barnabas).

Can you recognize how that informs our expectations of ministry? Let me suggest that we would be wisest to stay on script by preaching and teaching God's Word and not our political thoughts and practical musings. We all love a good story, and often they are helpful to illustrate a truth – but no church can survive on a Christian "Mark Twain" that offers a sermon of stories with little of God's Word. It may keep the crowd emotionally happy, but it will not grow them to be spiritually strong.

Expectation Two: We must anticipate building a team, seeking the spiritually sensitive, and giving a message from the Word of God.

Paphos Public Distractions

Barnabas, Paul and John Mark didn't stay long in Salamis, but made the more than 100 mile journey by Roman road to Paphos, where Luke pauses to add a story of the conversion of the Roman Proconsul Lucius Sergius Paulus:

*Acts 13:6 When they had gone through the whole island as far as **Paphos**, they found a magician, a Jewish false prophet whose name was Bar-Jesus, 7 who was with the proconsul, Sergius Paulus, a man of intelligence. This man summoned Barnabas and Saul and sought to hear the word of God. 8 But Elymas the magician (for so his name is translated) was opposing them, seeking to turn the proconsul away from the faith. 9 But Saul, who was also [known as] Paul, filled with the Holy Spirit, fixed his gaze on him, 10 and said, "You who are full of all deceit and fraud, you son of the devil, you enemy of all righteousness, will you not cease to make crooked the straight ways of the Lord? 11 "Now, behold, the hand of the Lord is upon you, and you will be blind and not see the sun for a time." And immediately a mist and a darkness fell upon him, and* *he went about seeking those who would lead him by the hand. 12 Then the proconsul believed when he saw what had happened, being amazed at the teaching of the Lord.*

Barnabas, Paul and John Mark came for the expressed purpose to share the Gospel and build discipleship circles that would initiate local churches. God sent them – that was clear in the text. Yet, the enemy didn't LEAVE because he heard the message of the Gospel was about to pour in – he set up confusion and conflict ahead of their arrival. That isn't unusual, it is the norm.

Expectation Three: We should anticipate the confusing words of the deceiver to try to "douse" those we attempt to reach. Sometimes outreach will include direct answers to those who are deliberately being deceptive.

Some Christians believe that one can only "play nicely" with others in their presentation – and certainly believers are to strive for peace. At the same time, failing to contend for the hearts of those who are lost is surrender to deception.

When our schools insist on representing naturalism as the only truth, and wrap it in a scientific lab coat – we will respond. We will tell them that they are betraying the foundation of the country in which we have enjoyed mutual blessing. Our fathers knew that our rights didn't come from government, but we God given an inalienable – they said so. "It is the duty of all nations to acknowledge the providence of Almighty God, to obey His will, to be grateful for His benefits, and humbly to implore His protection and favor," said George Washington. Yet that won't be at the core of our argument – the Bible will. We will continue to press for the truth of the Gospel and the place of the Word in the lives of students. Teaching western history while ignoring the influence of the Scriptures is a rouse strategically planned in modern education. We don't want conflict, but we won't surrender the Word for a peace that damns those without the truth. Expecting no conflict in sharing truth ignores the story God presented in the Book of Acts.

Perga Disappointments

From Paphos, the men set sail almost due north for a distance of about 175 miles to the landing near Perga, and then made their way into the town:

Acts 13:13 Now Paul and his companions put out to sea from Paphos and came to **Perga in Pamphylia***; but John left them and returned to Jerusalem.*

Yet, later Paul recalled the first entry to the region of greater Galatia as one in which he struggled physically (some scholars believe the Galatian letter embraced the entire area of central Anatolia, and there is ample evidence that he named the region but meant a broader territory):

Galatians 4:13 but you know that it was because of a bodily illness that I preached the gospel to you the first time; 14 and that which was a trial to you in my bodily condition you did not despise or loathe, but you received me as an angel of God, as Christ Jesus [Himself]. 15 Where then is that sense of blessing you had? For I bear you witness that, if possible, you would have plucked out your eyes and given them to me.

The mission team went through a time of division, and (it appears) physical weakness. I believe that John Mark didn't simply leave because he got homesick. I don't think he was simply young and inexperienced and unaccustomed to the size of the Taurus mountains the team was about to embark on crossing. Those things may have been true, but I don't think any of them were the deciding factor for why John left a hole in the team that later ruptured into an argument that broke the team up.

What was his problem? I think Paul said tough things to Elymas, and that surprised John Mark, and may have rattled him a bit. I think that Paul got sick and wasn't doing well, and that eroded the confidence in the team that John began with. That may be why Paul reacted so strongly later, just as a team for the second mission journey was coming together. Coming inland, Barnabas and Paul were hurt by the loss of John Mark – and it got between their relationship.

Expectation Four: We shouldn't anticipate a team without disappointment and conflict – that is part of God's story from the first journey. People on the team will let us down, and we must be ready for it. Our hope is in the Lord and His Word, not in the vessels that transport it to the world.

Pisidian Preaching

Moving inland, Barnabas and Paul made their way to Pisidian Antioch, gained a large audience, and began to preach to the Jews of that town. The account is long, so we will offer an overview of Paul's six point message:

*Acts 13:14 But going on from Perga, they arrived at **Pisidian Antioch**, and on the Sabbath day they went into the synagogue and sat down. 15 After the reading of the Law and the Prophets the synagogue officials sent to them, saying "Brethren, if you have any word of exhortation for the people, say it." 16 Paul stood up, and motioning with his hand said, "Men of Israel, and you who fear God, listen:*

God was at work in our collective Jewish past (13:17-22)

- He chose us and set us free from Egypt (17)
- He brought us through the wilderness (18)
- He cleared Canaanites off the land of our inheritance (19)
- He provided Judges until Samuel (20)
- He provided Kings – including Saul and David (21-22a)
- He gave a promise to King David (22b)

God is at work in our day (13:23-26)

- He sent His promised Savior – raising Him from the dead (23)
- He sent the announcer before Him – John the Baptizer (24-25)
- He sent US to YOU – to announce the message of salvation (26)

You cannot look to Jerusalem for the answer (13:27-32)

- They refused Him and rejected Him (27)
- They gave Him to Romans for execution (28)
- He was killed, but He was raised (29)!
- God was at work in that tomb (30)
- Many people witnessed Him risen and walking among us (31)
- We declare HE was the delivered of the promise of God (32)

You can confirm our message in the Scriptures (13:33-37)

The message is the total forgiveness of sins to those who believe – atonement has been replaced by justification (13:38-39)

Don't walk past your opportunity to respond to God's message (13:40-41).

From the moment of the delivery of their message, response and reaction began. Gentile proselytes (followers of Judaism who were not born Jews) begged for more information and kept following Paul and Barnabas (13:42-43). Unbelieving Jews resisted, became jealous and argumentative (13:45) and pushed Paul and Barnabas to spend more time with Gentile converts until they were pushed out of the area (13:46-51). The missionaries left behind in the region followers of Jesus who were joyful in spite of the pressures (13:52).

Expectation Five: We should not measure the work too early. Some of our engagements are to plant seed and will not bear the fruit we anticipate quickly. Our work is faithfulness, God's work is found in the results.

Iconium Plots

They pushed on to Iconium:

Acts 14:1 **In Iconium they entered the synagogue** of the Jews together, and spoke in such a manner that **a large number of people believed**, both of Jews and of Greeks. 2 But the Jews who **disbelieved stirred** up the minds of the Gentiles and embittered them against the brethren. 3 Therefore they spent a long time [there] speaking boldly [with reliance] upon the Lord, who was testifying to the word of His grace, **granting that signs and wonders be done by their hands**. 4 But the **people of the city were divided**; and some sided with the Jews, and some with the apostles. 5 And when an **attempt** was made by both the Gentiles and the Jews with their rulers, **to mistreat and to stone them, 6 they became aware of it and fled** to the cities of Lycaonia,

Lystra and Derbe, and the surrounding region; 7 and there they continued to preach the gospel.

Just when they were getting real response by a larger crowd, the opposition rose and became personal and dangerous. God empowered them with signs and wonders, but they knew when a plot was uncovered they should get out of town.

Expectation Six: Just because we carry God's Word doesn't mean we go in unwise of the atmosphere. Boldness is not stupidity.

We must be wise as serpents and harmless as doves. There is no real ministry without conflict – because the enemy will not surrender the field of battle without a fight.

Lystra Confusion and Anger

They went on from Iconium to Lystra and Derbe. Luke picked up one anecdote from the trip that summarized the problems encountered:

*Acts 14:8 **At Lystra a man was sitting who had no strength in his feet**, lame from his mother's womb, who had never walked. 9 This man was listening to **Paul** as he **spoke**, who, when he had fixed his gaze on him and had seen that he had faith to be made well, 10 said with a loud voice, "**Stand upright on your feet**." And he leaped up and [began] to walk. 11 When the crowds saw what Paul had done, they raised their voice, saying in the Lycaonian language, "**The gods have become like men and have come down to us**." 12 And they [began] calling Barnabas, Zeus, and Paul, Hermes, because he was the chief speaker. 13 The priest of Zeus, whose [temple] was just outside the city, brought oxen and garlands to the gates, and wanted to offer sacrifice with the crowds. 14 But when the apostles Barnabas and Paul heard of it, they tore their robes and rushed out into the crowd, crying out 15 and saying,*

"Men, why are you doing these things? We are also men of the same nature as you, and preach the gospel to you that you should turn from these vain things to a living God, WHO MADE THE HEAVEN AND THE EARTH AND THE SEA AND ALL THAT IS IN THEM. 16 "In the generations gone by He permitted all the nations to go their own ways; 17 and yet He did not leave Himself without witness, in that He did good and gave you rains from heaven and fruitful seasons, satisfying your hearts with food and gladness." 18 [Even] saying these things, with difficulty they restrained the crowds from offering sacrifice to them. 19 But Jews came from Antioch and Iconium, and having won over the crowds, they stoned Paul and dragged him out of the city, supposing him to be dead. 20 But while the disciples stood around him, he got up and entered the city. The next day he went away with Barnabas to Derbe.

No sooner had Paul brought the truth of Jesus which was validated by a sign miracle, the people were led into a "side street" of faith. They became fixated on the power, and dropped the message of Jesus into the end of their paganism.

Expectation Seven: People will always be tempted to add Jesus to their pagan lifestyle and modify the message of surrender.

They want eternal life and a relationship with God – but they want to keep their old ways of seeing the world. That defines the battle line of the message – surrender is what God is looking for from people. Jesus won't be added to a formula of other answers to life.

Derbe Calm and the Return Pass

The end of the passage tells of the return and offers a very important detail…

*Acts 14:21 After they had preached the gospel to that city and had made many disciples, they returned to Lystra and to Iconium and to Antioch, 22 **strengthening the souls** of the disciples, encouraging them to continue in the faith, and [saying], "**Through many tribulations we must enter the kingdom of God.**" 23 When they had **appointed elders for them in every church**, having prayed with fasting, they commended them to the Lord in whom they had believed. 24 They passed through Pisidia and came into Pamphylia. 25 When they had spoken the word in Perga, they went down to Attalia. 26 From there they sailed to Antioch, from which they had been commended to the grace of God for the work that they had accomplished. 27 When they had arrived and gathered the church together, they [began] to report all things that God had done with them and how He had opened a door of faith to the Gentiles. 28 And they spent a long time with the disciples.*

Groups of believers were revisited. They were encouraged, but not with the fluff of some guarantee of peace, prosperity and safety. They were told that it would be TOUGH to follow God. Not left to flounder around, leadership was appointed and churches were formed. Before they had a Bible study – with leadership and accountability structure it became a **church**.

Expectation Eight: Sustainable ministry isn't just about sharing the Gospel or promising people Heaven – it is about building accountability structures in the body of Christ that can help people navigate the hard times we face in this world.

Let me close this lesson on expectations by reminding you of something that, by now, may be incredibly obvious. **People are going to fail us because fallen people hurt each other**. We must construct in our lives the proper mechanisms to forgive them. Yet, real forgiveness doesn't begin with focusing on the people who hurt me. I must first deal in my heart with God – and my deep desire to hold on to the wrong until I feel the satisfaction of justice. Bitterness is a reflection that I don't trust God to make things right in His time. When I release the wrong committed against me into God's hands, I begin to gain the ability to forgive the one who wounded me. My forgiveness then, starts between me and God, and the healing between me and another is the effect of that – it is not the primary focus.

God's Word can help us reset expectations so that we can navigate life thoughtfully and positively as individuals and as a Gospel movement.

Paul's Response to the Roman World:
"The Jerusalem Council: Fight Rules"

We have been investigating the Biblical record on the life and mission of Paul, the famous first century Apostle to the Gentile world. In this lesson, I want to talk about how something tough to deal with. The text of Acts now moves into the hard subject of fighting and interpersonal disagreements between believers – but the approach we are taking will not leave us cynical or angry. In fact, even dissention and division *can* become a positive stage from which we can learn critical lessons about our walk with God. To be fair, our subject was not CHOSEN by me, it is the subject recorded as the next major hurdle Paul had to pass over in becoming effective as a church planter. This was the situation: Acts 15 recorded the minutes of a tough meeting of the elders of the early church as they came together to settle a critical dispute in a divided room of the early church. This became one of the most important learning settings for Paul in his early missionary days. Why? **Because handling conflict is a critical function of any good leader** – and Paul was being shaped by God. The record of this shaping is found in the account of an argument by men of God who were struggling to discern God's direction during the infancy of the church movement. Though I am certain there were **many disagreements and disputes** among followers of Jesus in that time, this one was preserved for our understanding because it was deemed by God to be critical to the growth of the church and its leaders.

Let's face it, **men have been fighting since Cain killed Abel**, but it took many centuries for them to apply actual "rules" to physical conflict and call it a "sport." What the Greeks first called "pygmachia" (now called "boxing") can probably be traced back to the seventh century BCE (during the period of the divided kingdom in Israel and Judah) when the combat sport made its debut in the Olympic games. The idea was to place two people in a cordoned area and allow them to strike one another with blows using leather strapped fists (which were eventually replaced by gloves). As a "sport" this "prize fighting" grew and became more organized over the centuries, but became largely popularized in the eighteenth and nineteenth centuries first in Britain, then in the US. As its popularity increased, so did formalization of the rules around which a sanctioned fight took place. Today, the Olympian boxers learn a great number of rules that specify when and where a punch can be thrown. Even beyond physical fighting, the Greeks **also left the west a legacy of a type of verbal sparring** now referred to simply as "debate." It also has come of age with many rules, though in its political and social media forms such rules are hard to discern. I mention these forms of "fighting" because they illustrate the idea of sparring with rules.

Here is the truth: **Believers must come to recognize that not everyone who follows Jesus agrees with one another on a host of issues – so conflict isn't unnatural.** In fact, I believe the text will show that God uses even conflict between believers to sharpen each other in truth – though I readily admit the process is difficult, painful and often distracting to other ministry objectives. **It is essential that we learn how to handle disagreement in a godly way, and for that God gave us the record of a model dispute.** He intended us to know how to successfully navigate even intense disagreements between believers, including those on the most sensitive of issues. How can we pass through these disputes successfully? Is there a key? Yes...

Key Principle: The key to settling disputes is not the agreement to the debated issue, but agreement to the contract that both sides will follow the system set up for arbitration, and ultimately support the decision of the designated leadership.

That's a lot of verbiage. The point is simple: in order for a dispute to be settled and peace restored to a divided situation, people have to agree on the METHOD of settling the dispute and the AUTHORITIES that should do so. If such an agreement is not made, the issue will leave the church fractured. Let's look at the model, and see what God taught Paul (and will teach us) from the struggle:

Division on the Field

The passage opened with a visit from some Jewish men of the Jerusalem area:

Acts 15:1 Some men came down from Judea and [began] teaching the brethren, "Unless you are circumcised according to the custom of Moses, you cannot be saved." 2 And when Paul and Barnabas had great dissension and debate with them, [the brethren] determined that Paul and Barnabas and some others of them should go up to Jerusalem to the apostles and elders concerning this issue. 3 Therefore, being sent on their way by the church, they were passing through both Phoenicia and Samaria, describing in detail the conversion of the Gentiles, and were bringing great joy to all the brethren. 4 When they arrived at Jerusalem, they were received by the church and the apostles and the elders, and they reported all that God had done with them. 5 But some of the sect of the Pharisees who had believed stood up, saying, "It is necessary to circumcise them and to direct them to observe the Law of Moses." 6 The apostles and the elders came together to look into this matter.

First, note the issue was raised by Judean visitors (better explained in verse 5). They argued (paraphrasing): "To be saved, Gentiles must become Jewish proselytes – beginning with circumcision and moving into the instruction of the Torah" (15:1,5). They represented the accepted norm in Judaism, and there was little reason to believe that God had changed the situation based on what THEY knew of the issues. What they were saying had been said for centuries – and in the past it was both Biblically accurate and (of course) ethically sound.

Next, we should take note that even in the most critical areas of the faith, there was disagreement. In a tolerance laden culture we must remember that not everyone can be right, but disagreement doesn't need to lead to destruction - there is a way to deal with differences. How do we bring a serious and divisive issue to agreement and peace? The model offers help:

First, we must recognize the division and define the issues. This is a critical beginning to the solution. We cannot solve an issue we cannot define. Look at the model…

Initially it caused two parties to develop, opening debate and **confusing the core of the Gospel message** (15:2): The issue was defined as whether salvation came to anyone simply by God's grace through the respondent's faith. Did the message of the Gospel mean an end to the need for atonement (replacing it with justification)? If that sentiment was true, a man or woman's participation in attaining cleansing was greatly curtailed. They didn't need to raise a sacrificial animal, nor did they need to stand in the long lines for slaughter of that animal. They didn't need to make the trip to Jerusalem at times of sacrifice. Any Jew would recognize the startling implications for the center of the faith's observance! In this way, the fear of losing the center played into the theology of the people of Judea. Seeking the critical issues will force us to think clearly about our positions and their implications- but it will also help us define our fears.

Second, if we follow their example, we should get the best minds available and most informed people to offer evidence. These weren't just smart people in the room, but people who KNEW GOD and had a walk with God. Stop for a second and look at what the men did to gather information, because it is a critical part of the Acts record (cp. 15:2). I am going to camp here for a few minutes, because this part gets overlooked too often...

In the model, the **church sent men to gain clarification with evidence of what was being presented.** Paul and Barnabas could testify to the idea that God was at work among the Gentiles without their participation in the atonement system of Temple Judaism. As a result, the team was allowed to share their experiences from their travels and what God appeared to be doing from what they experienced (15:3-4). **Yet, their experience NEEDED TO BE CHECKED AGAINST OTHER ISSUES.**

Don't skip this part! The "testimony gathering" stage was not inconsequential for Jerusalem's council, nor was the hearing small to Paul and Barnabas. Leaders make decisions based on facts – not simply voiced fears. By getting first hand testimony, **Jerusalem properly collected anecdotes that would help them make the right decision** – but by seeking Jerusalem's counsel on the experience, **Paul and Barnabas showed respect for a proper decision making process** for the churches.

Stop for a moment and see if you can recognize one of the great issues of our day at this point in our study. For many in the modern church, **personal experience too often dictates the determination of truth**. If you are younger than 30 years of age, there are two critical lies that have been subtly introduced into many serious discussions of moral behavior. They have often been introduced by educators and further reinforced by modern entertainers.

- First is the idea that **moral premises can be decided on the basis of your personal feelings alone**.

- Second is the notion that your **life experience is the best guide for truth**. True Christian thinking, i.e. Biblical thinking stands opposed to both ideas.

To the first, a **Christian acknowledges that how I feel about things needs to be subjected to how *GOD* feels about them**, and that is clear only when I understand what the Bible truly says about the issue at the center of my decision. I cannot be "taking up a cross daily and following Jesus" while openly opposing God's right to set the standard of behavior for His created beings.

To the second, followers of Jesus must **reckon that our grasp of experience is grossly limited because we only perceive PART of what is truly happening**. We are passing through an experience that we will only truly understand much later.

Here is the key: **Decisions about truth and reckoning of moral behavior are not reliably decided based on feeling and experience apart from the Biblical record**. Such standards of behavior are not Christian. They are pagan, ungodly and strongly applauded by a fallen world. When the whole fallen world is for your "boldly tolerant" decision, you should not be impressed. Open your Bible; therein is the standard for the follower of Jesus.

The fact is that Bible believers, when living Biblically, confound the modern way of thinking because they can both **love the person they see as living in an immoral way** and yet **reject their life behavior as wrong**. I don't *hate* people who oppose the Biblical view; I see them as *victims* of the "Fall of man", held in the embrace of a fallen prince doomed to destruction. They aren't the *problem* to be solved; they are the *sinner* to be loved. **At the same time, I will not embrace their standard of behavior no matter how bigoted they evaluate my faith to be.** Why? Because if there is a God (as the Bible purports) and if this IS His standard (in the Bible), how they feel about my evaluation of their life is not more compelling to me than what HE has said about their behavior. If I surrender that ground, I have surrendered the Bible to the modern sense of toleration, and I have no message for the sinner but this: "God loves you, but do what you want, or what seems good to you." That isn't Biblical at all, and it robs the church of a message that God will save you from your fallen state.

Increasingly, as the culture changes to make what the Bible defines as wrong into a "civil right," we are **forced** to do this. Let me be clear: **Our experiences with people must not determine our standard of behavior – that is offered by our Creator in His Word**. That is one of the things that makes a Christian a follower of Christ. We do NOT simply follow some vaguely formed "love and tolerance" Jesus message – we read the whole of the book and seek to recognize the actual textual principles of it – which are considerably detailed in the 1189 chapters of the Bible. Some in our society boil the message of Jesus into a tolerance that accepts all behaviors – but that doesn't match the text at all.

For older believers who engage this lesson, you may not understand why I am slowing down to examine this part of the story...but this is critical to our young. I strongly believe we are living in a day of delusion -even within the community of the Christian faith. Many begin with the flawed foundational idea that God's chief interest is their happiness (not holiness). Because of that, anything that would curtail their ability to express their inner desires and feelings could not be commanded by this "reshaped" god they now follow. **If they feel they were "made with certain desires," they cannot imagine a god that would tell them to deny their feelings – because their true god is their appetite.** We live in a time where even believers have been subtly convinced that the center of the universe is how they feel, not Who they serve – and that separates the modern church from the message of its past.

The point is simple: **How I feel about things needs to be subjected to how GOD feels about them**:

- Do I feel sex outside of marriage is wrong? The *Christian* answer is "Who cares what you feel about that?" The believer may feel it is perfectly *acceptable* in their heart ("because I really love them") – but the Bible makes it clear that it is NOT God's standard. When weighing the deciding factor, Christian thinking dictates that God's Word is the standard of both my faith *and* my behavior.

- Do I feel that because someone says: "I have always felt this way," that acting on that feeling is ok with God? The Biblical answer is "Your feelings are from a fallen heart that will deceive you." That is what the Bible teaches.

In the problem in Acts, anecdotal experience was presented, but it wasn't the deciding factor. A thousand experiences from the testimony of the internet may be a tool for clarity, but only if we know how to filter properly the critical issues of the debate. Let me be pointed here:

A young woman I know well says she is a believer in Jesus. She decided to walk away from both her family and Biblical teaching given to her in her spiritual walk early in life. She wanted to be loved, and decided to sleep with a boyfriend outside of marriage and ended up living with him in a home with a whole group of others. She got pregnant – not once, but several times. The babies came one after another – but her boyfriend's sense of responsibility didn't keep a roof over her head, and her sexual escapades in those years didn't protect her from HIV. Now she is sick and frustrated because she is unable to offer her children any of her buried Biblical ideals in that deconstructed and immoral environment. As she has grown sicker, she realizes that her feelings that she "loved him" were not enough to make life work. She recognizes her limited life experience didn't anticipate the outcomes. Now she needs those who love her unconditionally – the family she walked away from - but the feelings that led her decisions did not take into account the rest of the people in her life who were passing through profound heartbreak because of each of her choices. They knew God's Word, and they saw it all coming. Don't be deceived – ungodly living leads to destroyed lives. With each of her ungodly, immoral and destructive decisions she sank deeper, but the modern world applauded, until the results came due. Her inexperience and her heart-led choices have created a mess for her child – but she couldn't see that when she decided on her lifestyle. Now, it is very probable that the state will have more children to raise for parents that "followed their heart" instead of their Bible.

Go back to the Jerusalem Council. Look at the third way they worked to solve the issue. They defined the issue, they gathered the facts... what was next? Since they knew the problems could not be settled by people on the scene, they sought help. **Third, they took the problem to those who are experts and authorities in the issue.**

At Jerusalem, some Pharisees objected (15:5) so the council came to consider the issue (15:6). Nothing is served by shutting out one view before the hearing. **They let those who objected speak, even if they are not in the majority.**

Debate **between** Delegates

Listen for a moment to the debate in the room:

*Acts 15:7 After there had been much debate, Peter stood up and said to them, "Brethren, you know that in the early days God made a choice among you, that by my mouth the Gentiles would hear the word of the gospel and believe. 8 "And God, who knows the heart, testified to them giving them the **Holy Spirit**, just as He also did to us; 9 and **He made no distinction between us and them, cleansing their hearts by faith**. 10 "Now* *therefore why do you put God to the test by placing upon the neck of the disciples a yoke which neither our fathers nor we have been able to bear? 11 "But we believe that **we are saved through the grace of the Lord Jesus, in the same way as they also are**." 12 All the people kept silent, and they were listening to **Barnabas and Paul as they were relating what signs and wonders God had done** through them among the Gentiles.*

First, people got the chance to speak from their experiences, their feelings and their best understandings. No one knows everything, so the debate probably changed some positions in the room. This wasn't the modern form of yelling and sarcasm that debate has become – this was scholarly determination, with pliable and teachable hearts of men who respected one another and cared deeply for one another. When people don't care about one another, the debate degrades quickly into a shouting match.

After some debate, Peter took the floor and began to share his experiences that seemed inexplicable apart from a "God at work" moment. He noted the time he stood before Cornelius and made clear he didn't see God's move coming. He made clear that God didn't seem to distinguish between Jew and Gentile in the move of the Spirit's gifts. He also made clear that he didn't want to press the Gentiles into the atonement system – because keeping one's eternal state was a heavy business that often led to failure. After that testimony came the moment that probably swayed a number of hearts. Peter said: "Either we believe that justification apart from any human work is the Gospel, or we don't."

There is was: the clear choice was made plain. The Gospel would either be that Gentiles could become Jews (a message that had been around for centuries), or the Gospel was that justification (total repair of the formerly broken relationship with God) was available to anyone who would believe that Jesus paid it all for them. Paul and Barnabas sided with the latter notion, and gave testimony as to how that was clearly working in the Gentile world.

Determination of the Council

It was time to decide. James (who headed the council) spoke to the issue:

*Acts 15:13 After they had stopped speaking, James answered, saying, "Brethren, listen to me. 14 "**Simeon has related** how God first concerned Himself about taking from among the Gentiles a people for His name. 15 "With this the words of the **Prophets agree**, just as it is written, 16 AFTER THESE THINGS I will return, AND I WILL REBUILD THE TABERNACLE OF DAVID WHICH HAS FALLEN, AND I WILL REBUILD ITS RUINS, AND I WILL RESTORE IT, 17 SO THAT THE REST OF MANKIND MAY SEEK THE LORD, AND ALL THE GENTILES WHO ARE CALLED BY MY NAME,' 18 SAYS THE LORD, WHO MAKES THESE THINGS KNOWN FROM LONG AGO. 19 "**Therefore it is my judgment** that we **do not trouble** those who are turning to God from among the **Gentiles**, 20 but that we **write to them** that they **abstain** from things contaminated by **idols** and from **fornication** and from what is **strangled** and from **blood**. 21 "For **Moses** from ancient generations has in every city those who preach him, since he is **read** in the **synagogues** every Sabbath." 22 Then it **seemed good to the apostles and the elders**, with the whole church, to **choose men** from among them to send to Antioch with Paul and Barnabas-- Judas called Barsabbas, and Silas, leading men among the brethren, 23 and they **sent this letter** by them..." The rest of the passage is about the letter repeating the words of James, and the men moving out with the letter that contained the words...*

Obviously, the church needed **clarity**, and **there was a system for caring for the problem**. What was **key** in these verses is the line of reasoning used to solve the issue:

James **cited the testimony** of the trusted men about their experience (Acts 15:14) – but that was not the deciding factor. His decision, as our decision in any moral or doctrinal issue, was based on the how the idea or behavior fit the **Scriptural frame** already exposed by God in His Word.

James **showed sensitivity to all sides of the debate**, but he took a stand. In our modern culture of tolerance, that may sound JUDGY, but not everyone is right when two moral or behavioral codes run in opposite directions. James made clear the teaching in four statements:

- They must **set aside life in the pagan temple** – no small affair for an ingrained Roman citizen.
- They must **not eat blood**.
- They must **not eat animals that have been killed by strangulation** nor participate in the pagan services that do such things.
- They must **forsake sexual sin** and walk in purity (something associated with pagan ritual as well as standard Roman practice).

James recognized the **differences that God maintained** – not everyone was going to be doing the same thing to be in obedience to God's call for them. Many Christians lose track of the issues in this passage. James was NOT telling Jews not to circumcise nor keep Sabbath – that wasn't his point. He made the decision "Concerning Gentiles" not changing anything for the Jewish people at that point. Much later in Acts 21:20, it will become clear that Jews keeping the Law was not in view in the decision making process at all.

It is NOT Biblical to think that any distinction in the functions of people fundamentally demeans people. The Bible made clear that men and women were given differing roles by God – but both are equally valued by God. Jews and Gentiles were given differing standards of food and drink, dress and celebration by God – but that doesn't mean that one was viewed as superior to the other. Modern thinking has assaulted this value system, claiming that anything that distinguished one person from another demeans people.

Telling women they are not to pastor a church is not the same thing as making an African-American sit in the back of a bus. One was the action of people who made another subservient to them out of a misguided and evil sense of superiority; the other is a statement based on overwhelming evidence from the Bible itself. Believers can disagree on the meaning of those passages (though I believe they are quite clear), but we must recognize that adherence to that standard is not intended to be mean spirited.

It is always Biblically immoral to demean anyone's value (since that value is tied up in their creation by a Majestic God), but it is NOT wrong to limit one's desired behaviors based on what the Bible expressly teaches. That was part of the POINT of God's reveal truth – to transform us and change our behaviors from their fallen desires.

The issue was solved, and the council sorted out the complex arguments and **boiled down the action steps** for the group, showing public agreement.

Delivery to the Perplexed

The letter was carried, and the small house churches were **completely informed** on the issue and the decision.

Acts 15:30 So when they were sent away, they went down to Antioch; and having gathered the congregation together, they delivered the letter..."

Here is my question: "Why did this work?" I believe the answer is this: "Some **vital points of agreement** were understood at the beginning. They LOVED one another, and respected men of God that showed His leading in their lives listened to one another carefully. Yet, there was something more: Both sides accepted the process and showed respect for their leaders, when those leaders lived and taught in a way that reflected God's Word.

Our text dealt with three basic questions about disagreements in the body:

When was contention necessary? (15:1) It must come when the issue is essential to the core message of the group, there must be agreement (15:1). These were not contentions over style or preference – but essential truths that made fellowship impossible without agreement.

What was the process of dealing with serious disagreements? (15:2-5) In a "face to face" meeting, people presented their understandings to the other (15:2a), set aside their ego, and met with congeniality and care.

How did the council decide the truth concerning the opposing views? (15:6-35). First, they accepted evidence that God was at work. Though experiential, that evidence was one of the ways the church could see the hand of God in their lives. (15:7-12). Then they related any experiences to the filter of the Word of God (15:13-18). Finally, when the decision was made, they publically supported it.

The key to settling disputes is not the agreement to the debated issue, but agreement to the contract that both sides will follow the system set up for arbitration, and ultimately support the decision of the designated leadership.

Paul, like all of the men in the room, walked away refreshed with God's work through the whole room. He learned a pattern that would serve him well – because conflict would occur more than he could possibly know in the days ahead.

Paul's Response to the Roman World: "The Second Mission Journey: Long Hot Summer"

Some movie buffs will recall that all the way back in 1958; actor Paul Newman (before he was making terrific jars of spaghetti sauce for our local supermarkets) played a role in a film based on William Faulkner's short stories called: "The long hot summer." I confess I didn't see the film – but I read the series of Faulkner's short stories that were connected to the film, and a summary of how the screenwriter wove them together, and I was fascinated. Apparently, in the movie a drifter named Ben Quick (played by Newman) entered a small Mississippi town where his father had a bad reputation as an arsonist. A town leader played by Orson Welles held a grudge against Ben's dad, and went after the young man to make life difficult for him. Over time, that harsh community leader developed a muted respect for Ben's tenacity in the face of countless obstacles, especially in light of that town leader's own flighty and over privileged son. Eventually the town leader tried to fix Ben up with his own daughter, but his wicked son began to fear he would lose his place as heir and trapped his father in a barn, lighting a fire and planting evidence implicating Ben. The movie was called "The Long Hot Summer" because it reflected a tough time in young Ben's life – and showed his tenacity and ability to rebound in spite of setbacks.

Americans *love* these kinds of stories. We love self-made, self-repairing men supermen. We have a mild *contempt* for defeat, and if not overtly, we secretly love a guy who can get off the canvas when knocked down and go on to win the fight. The problem is, **sometimes you can't win**. Sometimes the forces against you are too strong to make it through by "toughing it out." Even in our spiritual life, **times will come when we need help** if we are going to have victory. We were not designed to take on life's obstacles in the spiritual realm without each other, without God's Word, and without times of rest and protection from the buffeting of the spiritual elements.

Some people are surprised when they read the section found in Acts 15:36-18:23 – what is dubbed the "**Second Mission Journey of Paul**" – because a close reading doesn't reveal the "spotless" and "Teflon" version of Paul they have been taught to imagine. Paul gets beaten worse than Rocky Balboa in a boxing ring. Dr. Luke took the time to remind us, fully under the direction of God's Spirit; of the time when Paul probably considered quitting because the work wasn't going well at all. It got **so bad** he despaired and couldn't continue to function normally. The record of this journey reveals that God was faithful and moved him from pain to power. It is certainly a process we should investigate!

Key Principle: When life pummels even the strongest believer with defeats, there is a process God can use to rebuild them – but that believer must take advantage of the provision.

Instead of reading every verse for nearly three chapters, I will need to select the ones that help move the story. I am not suggesting that every word is not important, and in other lessons we have studied each chapter, line by line. For this lesson, however, what we want to look at requires an overview – a look at the forest and not the individual trees on the landscape. Start with the end of the Jerusalem Council, where we left off in the last lesson:

Acts 15:36 After some days Paul said to Barnabas, "Let us return and visit the brethren in every city in which we proclaimed the word of the Lord, [and see] how they are." 37 Barnabas wanted to take John, called Mark, along with them also. 38 But Paul kept insisting that they should not take him along who had deserted them in Pamphylia and had not gone with them to the work. 39 And there occurred such a sharp disagreement that they separated from one another, and Barnabas took

Mark with him and sailed away to Cyprus. 40 But Paul chose Silas and left, being committed by the brethren to the grace of the Lord. 41 And he was traveling through Syria and Cilicia, strengthening the churches.

Put yourself in Paul's toga and sandals. After a mammoth wrestling match at the council, the Spirit gave direction. The men embraced and the air was sweet with unity…but it didn't last.

Division in the Team

Did you ever have an argument with someone you love, but you feel like they were DEAD WRONG about what they said. Tell the truth: "Did you not go over the conversation scores of times in your head?" If you answered "Yes!", you are able to think like Paul as he and Silas boarded the ship and sailed off on the journey. Jesus was raised about twenty years before, and the church had just dodged its first nearly fatal division, and now the mission team is breaking up. I am certain they put a good face on it with the classic: "God is simply leading us in different directions" theme – but I do not for a moment believe both Barney and Paul were leaving unscathed by the altercation. Pain clings and pain stings… and it isn't easy to shake it off…

Off they went, Silas and Paul. For a bit, things looked like they were turning around…

Acts 16:1 Paul came also to Derbe and to Lystra. And a disciple was there, named Timothy, the son of a Jewish woman who was a believer, but his father was a Greek, 2 and he was well spoken of by the brethren who were in Lystra and Iconium. 3 Paul wanted this man to go with him; and he took him and circumcised him because of the Jews who were in those parts, for they all knew that his father was a Greek. 4 Now while they were passing through the cities, they were delivering the decrees which had been decided upon by the apostles and elders who were in Jerusalem, for them to observe.

5 So the churches were being strengthened in the faith, and were increasing in number daily.

There's a bit of encouragement – the team got back to full strength. Tim joined and seemed teachable. Paul was anxious to have him join in, and wanted to invest in his life. He knew his momma was a Jew, and he took the place of his father and had the boy circumcised, because people knew he hadn't been with a Greek dad. They delivered the message of the council and people were enthusiastic! What a great moment... but wait for it... things were about to get hazy.

Disorientation of the Team

It seems that Paul and Silas wanted to go on to Galatia, but that wasn't God's plan. Look at Acts 16:

*Acts 16:6 They passed through the Phrygian and Galatian region, having been **forbidden by the Holy Spirit** to speak the word in Asia; 7 and after they came to Mysia, they were trying to go into Bithynia, and the **Spirit of Jesus did not permit** them; 8 and passing by Mysia, they came down to Troas.*

The mission team came with a brochure hot off the Jerusalem press. It worked well in Iconium and Lystra – but now... dead stop. God's Spirit said "NO!" to the journey north and east. No problem, how about "due north"? "No way!" Can you hear Tim saying: "Hey guys, um... is it always this confusing? Do you USUALLY have a plan?" Without direction, they decided it was nap time... so they turned in for the night.

Direction was renewed when Paul had a vision of a Macedonian man (Acts 16:9-10) and that set the agenda to head for a boat and cross over to Neapolis, bound for Philippi up the road (Acts 16:11-12). The place was thoroughly pagan and the Jewish community was so small it didn't have a synagogue, so every Jew in town naturally headed for the nearest stream to have what is called a "Taschlich" ceremony – and begin worship. Paul headed that direction as well. Acts 16 says:

Acts 16:13 And on the Sabbath day we went outside the gate to a riverside...14 A woman named Lydia, from the city of Thyatira, a seller of purple fabrics, a worshiper of God, was listening; and the Lord opened her heart to respond to the things spoken by Paul. 15 And when she and her household had been baptized, she urged us, saying, "If you have judged me to be faithful to the Lord, come into my house and stay." And she prevailed upon us.

Wow, now things are turning around! People are coming to Jesus, right? Not so fast...

Draining of the Team:

Acts 16 shared that they no sooner got the home invitation, and the enemy slid into the scene in the form of a possessed slave girl (Acts 16:16).

Acts 16:17 Following after Paul and us, she kept crying out, saying, "These men are bond-servants of the Most High God, who are proclaiming to you the way of salvation." 18 She continued doing this for many days. But Paul was greatly annoyed, and turned and said to the spirit, "I command you in the name of Jesus Christ to come out of her!" And it came out at that very moment.

Just as the hope of a new mission point was dawning, there was an incessant disruption to the ministry. If you read that Paul got ANNOYED you read the passage correctly. He couldn't take the constant haranguing. Out came the spirit, and down on Paul and Silas came the law! They were seized by the authorities (Acts 16:19-21). They were hastily and unlawfully beaten with rods (Acts 16:22) and put in prison with their feet in stocks (Acts 16:23-24).

What do you do when you have been unlawfully arrested and beaten? Paul and Silas thought it was a good time for a song service! Acts 16:25-34 tells of the marvelous way that Paul and Silas rocked the house with their praise band... Ok, that was a bad way to say it. Seriously, they worshipped and God worked. An earthquake opened the door of the cell, but the testimony of Paul and Silas opened the door of a jailer's heart – and God saved the Philippian jailer and his house. By the end of the chapter, our missionaries were escorted out of town, but the bruises were still on their bodies. Every sneeze made Silas' eyes well up with tears.

When the body gets beaten, the heart gets weak. Paul and Silas knew God was at work. They knew God used their heating to save Joe the Jailer (or whatever his name was). At the same time, that didn't mean that the beating didn't take its toll on them. It surely did. They went through a physically draining time, and left feeling like an elephant sat on them in the night.

Dried Out Hearts for the Dynamic Duo

They walked westward on the Via Egnatia, a well-built Roman highway constructed two hundred years before and kept very well by Rome. They passed Amphipolis and Apollonia, but stopped at Thessalonica, where Paul had family. The response was initially good in Acts 17:1-4, but you know you can hear a "but" coming in the story...

Acts 17:5 But the Jews, becoming jealous and taking along some wicked men from the market place, formed a mob and set the city in an uproar; and attacking the house of Jason, they were seeking to bring them out to the people. 6 When they did not find them, they [began] dragging Jason and some brethren before the city authorities, shouting, "These men who have upset the world have come here also; 7 and Jason has welcomed them, and they all act contrary to the decrees of

Caesar, saying that there is another king, Jesus." 8 They stirred up the crowd and the city authorities who heard these things. 9 And when they had received a pledge from Jason and the others, they released them.

Only a brief time of growing ministry was pounced upon by enemies of the Gospel, and Paul's cousin Jason was arrested and held on bond to force Paul to move out of town (Acts 17:5-9). This was no doubt an emotionally draining time. By the time Paul and Silas left town, their bodies were healing some, but their hearts couldn't have been at peace. The trip began with a split. Philippi left them with split lips, and Thessalonica left them with a split up family. If we were keeping track, I am not sure we would call this a "winning time" in the mission quest.

Distorted by the Personal Attack

Slipping away from Thessalonica so that Jason wouldn't grow old in jail, Paul and Silas left in the night to the city of Berea, and hoped for a better reception ahead (Acts 17:10). Berea had a good reputation for a great synagogue crowd (Acts 17:11) and the mission team got a good start. The problem was, that soon the same rabble rousers that bothered them in Thessalonica heard they were gaining ground in Berea, so in came the guys with the pitch-forks and placards, and the whole thing deteriorated. Look at Acts 17:13-15:

Acts 17:13 But when the Jews of Thessalonica found out that the word of God had been proclaimed by Paul in Berea also, they came there as well, agitating and stirring up the crowds. 14 Then immediately the **brethren sent Paul out to go as far as the sea**; *and Silas and Timothy remained there. 15 Now those who escorted Paul brought him as far as Athens; and receiving a command for Silas and Timothy to come to him as soon as possible, they left.*

Paul was not only getting chased by the same band, they picked HIM as the object of their derision. The TEAM was able to stay at Berea... but PAUL had to find the nearest boat at the nearby Dion harbor. Paul was clearly **singled out and told to leave**, while his companions would remain and sure up the work. The **personal nature** of the attack just as his gifts were igniting into results certainly left a mark on his feelings.

Ok, now put yourself on the boat with Paul. Travel alone for a bit. Your old team partner stormed off. You went through a down time and couldn't get God's direction. Your body hurts from rod beating. Your family has been attacked. You have been singled out as the central problem... and you have been doing your best to follow Jesus... but it doesn't seem to be working well...

Disillusioned and Alone

In the modern mythology of the church, some will be offended that I picture "St. Paul" as, well, a regular guy. I have walked every place he ministered, and I have been impressed with how Dr. Luke didn't exactly try to pretty up the story. Paul made his way to Athens... we don't know exactly how, but we do know what happened when he got there. The loneliness and idle time appeared to make Paul a bit anxious, and he was stirred as he saw the pagan centers of Athens. (Acts 17:16-18). Paul reasoned with the men from their own poetry, but did not use Scripture (Acts 17:28) – the **only time he did this on record**. His audience laughed and scorned him (though a few were saved – Acts 17:32-34). Listen to the end of Acts 17 and see if you can read Paul's feeling into the mix:

Acts 17:32 "Now when they heard of the resurrection of the dead, some [began] to sneer, but others said, "We shall hear you again concerning this." 33 So Paul went out of their midst. 34 But some men joined him and believed, among whom also were Dionysius the

Areopagite and a woman named Damaris and others with them. 18:1 After these things he left Athens and went to Corinth."

Did you notice how Acts 18:1 was short and to the point? It is as though Luke wanted us to know only this: "It didn't go so well, and he left, period."

Have you had enough? I hope so, because God doesn't leave His servants chewing dust and binding wounds without a purpose. God was about to open the air conditioned encouragement door, and Paul was in the blazing hot parking lot for as long as he could possible stand it. Remember this: God is always on time. He knows what we need, and He knows when we need it. Here comes restoration...

Devastated to Restored: Rehab

Some scholar point out that Paul recalled to the Corinthians later the low point of entry to them:

2 Corinthians 1:8 For we do not want you to be unaware, brethren, of our affliction which came [to us] in Asia, that we were burdened excessively, beyond our strength, so that we despaired even of life; 9indeed, we had the sentence of death within ourselves so that we would not trust in ourselves, but in God who raises the dead...

Paul admitted he was whipped when he got there. He was despairing, physically mentally and emotionally wiped out. Yet, God moved in to rescue him. In Acts 18:2-11 Luke offered a window on *how* God restored him:

First, God provided him a **team** to weave into (18:1-3)

Acts 18:2 And [Paul] he found a Jew named Aquila, a native of Pontus, having recently come from Italy with his wife Priscilla, because Claudius had commanded all the Jews to leave Rome. He came to them, 3 and because he was of the same trade, he stayed with them and they were working, for by trade they were tent-makers.

God brought into Paul's life, at the critical hour, people with natural connection to his life. They were both Jews, and both heavy cloth workers. The enemy's move to expel the Jews in Rome became Paul's opportunity to begin to heal. God has the ability to move people about in order to rebuild, restore and renew His people.

Second, God restored him to a work in a **place** he was strongest (18:4).

Acts 18:4 And he was reasoning in the synagogue every Sabbath and trying to persuade Jews and Greeks.

Paul went back to the place where his strengths could best be used – the place of debate in the synagogue. He had seen success there in the past, and it was a "natural habitat" for him.

Third, God **added back the balance of his team**, with exciting reports of God at work (18:5). When he faced opposition, he was surrounded by others who knew he was right (18:6).

Acts 18:5 But when Silas and Timothy came down from Macedonia, Paul [began] devoting himself completely to the word, solemnly testifying to the Jews that Jesus was the Christ. 6 But when they resisted and blasphemed, he shook out his garments and said to them, "Your blood [be] on your own heads! I am clean. From now on I will go to the Gentiles."

At long last, God sent back Silas and Tim – the team was reunited. Paul sent the men back and forth with some letters, but he took solace in their time together. There is NOTHING like familiar friends and family to help healing advance.

Fourth, God **added new believers** and new **successes** that helped him see God still at work in him (18:7-8).

Acts 18:7 Then he left there and went to the house of a man named Titius Justus, a worshiper of God, whose house was next to the synagogue. 8 Crispus, the leader of the synagogue, believed in the Lord with all his household, and many of the Corinthians when they heard were believing and being baptized.

Paul didn't gauge his life by numbers and success, but it was encouraging to have people respond to the message of Jesus, and grow in that ministry. God brought some key people to faith, and that lifted Paul's spirit!

Fifth, God **spoke directly to his pain**, and assured him that he had protection from God for his work (18:9-11)

Acts 18:9 And the Lord said to Paul in the night by a vision, "Do not be afraid [any longer], but go on speaking and do not be silent; 10 for I am with you, and no man will attack you in order to harm you, for I have many people in this city." 11 And he settled [there] a year and six months, teaching the word of God among them.

Nothing helped more than hearing from God directly. Jesus told him not to be afraid, recognizing the horrible stretch of ministry he had passed through. God gave Paul three very important gifts when he was beaten, but Paul had to recognize them:

- Still time: healing by working on known and waiting on unknown
- Special friends: healing by team strengthening
- Safe places: God put a hedge on him to heal him

The end of the journey contained a simple word that helps us know what really happened. In the face of the trouble, Paul made a vow to obey God. That consecration is tucked into a little detail of the Word in Acts 18:18 Paul, having remained many days longer, took leave of the brethren and put out to sea for Syria, and with him were Priscilla and Aquila. In Cenchrea he had his hair cut, for he was keeping a vow.

A strengthened Paul recommitted himself to God's work, no matter the cost.

When we strip away all the stories and drama – our lives come down to this: some things really hurt because we are trying to do right and things go very wrong. It hurts to put your trust in God and then have the rug pulled from beneath of us... but we must recognize that God hasn't left even when all seems to have fallen apart. He has given us resource in Him the world cannot understand because it does not possess.

There is an old story of a man who was shipwrecked on an island. He found no other people on the small island, but he did find a hut and much evidence that another had lived in the place before him. Beneath the hut was a store room full of food. In the hut there were many fine conveniences, but the man would not use the place or eat the food. The man kept a diary and wanted to survive without the help of anyone else – be they alive or not. His last entry in his diary revealed that he died exhausted and surrounded by the very provisions that would have saved his life...but he made his point. He didn't need anyone else. The only trouble is that the choice killed him.

Paul needed friends. He needed team members. He needed the reassurance of God's own words. He needed to use the provisions God made – and not fuss because things didn't seem to work out. It was his own weakness that allowed God to strongly use him.

When life pummels even the strongest believer with defeats, there is a process God can use to rebuild them – but that believer must take advantage of the provision.

Paul's Response to the Roman World: "The Writings from the Second Mission Journey: The First Letter to the Thessalonians"

For this lesson we leave the flow of Paul's travels and consider the beginning of his writing career. Paul and his team started the work at numerous churches – traveling from city to city and preaching the Gospel of salvation by faith in Jesus' work alone. Yet, I believe most followers of Jesus are more indebted to Paul for the works the Spirit of God used him to deliver – the thirteen epistles that bear his name, and other writings that may have been lost by God's sovereign direction. This lesson is about the first of Paul's letters, because this is where the letter falls in the story of his life. Strangely enough, when looking back to the first Thessalonian letter, I want to begin with a few words about a modern comedy screen play....

Carrie Fisher wrote a screenplay based on her own life in 1987 and by 1990 it was on the silver screen as a comedy movie called "Postcards from the Edge". In the year that followed, the movie was acclaimed at the Academy awards... The story was about an actress who was a recovering drug addict and her attempts to re-start her career and her life after leaving the treatment center. She was forced to move in with a "responsible adult" in order to keep her insurance, and she returned to take residence with a famous musical comedy star of the 1950s and '60s – her own mother. The title of the movie tells how "out of control" the scenes within the screenplay became – and I can only imagine on the big screen it was even *more* off the wall. I mention the screenplay because the title popped into my mind as soon as I began thinking through the letters to the Thessalonians...they were letters written from the edge of pain and during a season of recovery for Paul- and that often is forgotten in the teaching of the epistles to Thessalonica. Our next two lessons in the life of the Apostle will be about the substance of these letters.

You will recall that in our last study we saw that Paul was passing through a difficult time on that second mission journey, in part because the trip **began with an argument** that broke the

Paul and Barnabas team over the issue of John Mark. Next, they found themselves **confounded on God's direction** for forward progress, being stopped from heading toward Bithynia. God redirected the team with a dream of the Macedonian man, but Paul had no sooner seen his first converts there in Philippi, when he and Silas were **beaten and imprisoned**. After a dramatic release by God's intervention and then His providence, they passed through to Thessalonica – only to have **Paul's family member assaulted** (Jason) and held until Paul left town. On to Berea, and Paul saw success until a rabble had HIM singled out to depart alone for Athens. His **Athenian trip was "off script"** for Paul's normal venture, and as he continued to Corinth – he did so **extremely discouraged and beaten down**. It was during that short visit in Athens that Paul made the decision to dispatch Timothy to Thessalonica – delaying their reunion but offering Paul a window on the progress of the Gospel. As God helped Paul pick up the pieces he wrote the two letters to the Thessalonians help us grasp the mindset of Paul in recovery, and explore what was on his heart as God put him back together in Corinth. Paul showed that when wounded, a believer's values surface without "make up". People can see what we truly care about when we have no energy left to mask our broken heart.

Key Principle: A mature believer lives his values and follows under pressure, recognizing God is at work even when times are tough.

In these two lessons, we want to sweep quickly through the two letters Paul wrote and capture what was exposed of his heart by the letters. We know their **context**; now we need their **content**. The question we are seeking to answer is this: "What was exposed from the Apostle's heart as it was torn open by pain and tribulation over the rejection of the Gospel?" Let's focus on the First Epistle to the Thessalonians. The letter can be divided into two parts:

The Letter of Paul opened the letter with six declarations that recapped the context of the writing:

Paul exposed some important things by sharing simple declarations. Let's consider what we learn of him in each of the six:

First, it is obvious that Paul hurt:

Paul and his team was praying for the believers at Thessalonica constantly, thanking God for them, longing to return to them - but was hindered from going there (1:1-2; 2:17-20; 3:9-11).

Look at the phrases from 1 Thessalonians 1:2 **"We give thanks to God always for all of you,** *making mention of you* **in our prayers."** *Similar sentiments are expressed in 2:17 "But* **we,** *brethren, having been* **taken away from you** *for a short while—***in person, not in spirit**—*were all the more* **eager** *with great desire* **to see your face.** *18 For* **we wanted to come to you**—*I, Paul, more than once—and yet* **Satan hindered us."** *Later in 3:9 we read: "For what* **thanks** *can* **we render to God for you** *in return for all the joy with which we rejoice before our God on your account, 10 as we* **night and day** *keep* **praying** *most earnestly that* **we may see your face,** *and may* **complete what is lacking** *in your faith?"*

It is clear that when Paul's heart was torn open, what spilled out was his love for those other believers. Mature Christians care for younger believers – not to sit in judgment over them – but to see them progress. They communicate care for younger followers of Jesus, because the heart of the missionary isn't about self-affirmation but of love for lost men and women. That love doesn't end when they follow Christ – it morphs into a deeper and more permanent hope for their growth and life ahead.

Second, we see that Paul remembered:

Paul saw God's choice of them and their dramatic life changes by the power of the Spirit as they became followers of Jesus – the Gospel was obviously powerful among them (1:3-5; 2:13).

It is not difficult to see in places like 1 Thessalonians 1:3ff that Paul saw God at work in them. He wrote: "...5 for **our gospel** *did not* **come** *to you in word only, but* *also **in power** and in the Holy Spirit and **with** full **conviction**; just as **you know** what **kind of men we proved to be** among you for your sake." He affirmed that again in 2:13 "For this reason **we** also **constantly thank God** that when you received the word of God which you heard from us, **you accepted it** not **as** the word of men, but for what it really is, **the word of God**, which also performs its work in you who believe."*

How exciting to see God's hand touch lives. One of the rich assurances we have as we look back on ministry where we have been fortunate enough to participate is those times when we saw God heal a broken marriage that we couldn't fix with counsel. We stood amazed as God took a certain young man bent on self-destruction, and broke his life-hardened heart to lead him into his Creator's arms. It is one thing to know from God's Word that our both God *and* His message is powerful – it is another to experience God on the move. When it happened, Paul was deeply thankful God gave him a place in the room to watch what God was doing! The Apostle knew that excitement. Even in the brokenness of rejection by many in his present place, his heart remembered God at work in the past - and that kept him going.

Third, the Paul made the point that he promised some things:

Paul pledged that trouble would come, and it did quickly upon them as it had in his team's lives. They were afflicted and walking with God under fire, becoming witnesses to the world as they suffered injustice (1:6-8; 2:1-2; 3:4).

*Paul apparently never pulled his punches when he came to them initially. Perhaps preaching to people just after you have been beaten and jailed he figured, no sense trying to "pretty things up" – it was going to get tough quickly and he warned them. Note in 1 Thessalonians 1:6, he commended them when he wrote: "**You** also **became imitators** of us and of the Lord, **having received the word in much tribulation** with the joy of the Holy Spirit, 7 so that you **became an example** to all the believers **in Macedonia** and in*

*Achaia." He made clear the troubles of the mission team again in 1 Thessalonians 2:1-2, and reminded them in 3:4 "For indeed when we were with you, **we kept telling you** in advance that **we were going to suffer affliction**; and so it came to pass, as you know."*

I am continually amazed at how modern marketing has affected the presentation of the Gospel. Paul delivered a message that offered suffering and persecution from the outset. Where was the "how to have a happy and meaningful life" section? Paul's Gospel was about salvation from sin and a secure walk with God for eternity – not about a better bank account and other temporal perks. I recognize that our presentation needs to be culturally sensitive, but that cannot mean changing the substance of the truth because we want people to accept our message. I simply argue that when we change the message so drastically to grab our culture, what feed their self-focus, and betray the core of the message we were given to represent by God.

I personally think Paul marveled at how quickly they were "under the gun" in 1 Thessalonians 2:14:

*"For **you**, brethren, **became imitators of the churches of God in** Christ Jesus that are in **Judea**, for **you** also **endured the same sufferings** at the hands of your own countrymen, even **as they did from the Jews**, 15 who both killed the Lord Jesus and the prophets, and drove us out."*

What makes us think that we should preach to people prosperity with the signs of the times we see all about us? Why do we not accept the coming troubles as PART of our faith – after a long line of others have passed through similar things? Paul *promised* troubles with their belief, whether that hindered people from coming forward in the meeting or not. At least when trouble came, he could remind them of that promise. Will our churches be able to make the same claim if we preach a message of personal advancement?

Fourth, Paul clarified things about his motives:

Lest anyone attempt to charge that Paul's outreach was self-benefitting manipulation, Paul reminded them of how they offered truth in gentleness and love while working to be no burden to them (2:3-11).

*Attacks on Paul's preaching were evident from the start in the Book of Acts, and here Paul reinforced the content of some of those false charges. In 1 Thessalonians 2:3, Paul didn't defend himself beyond making clear the truth. He wrote: "For **our exhortation** does **not** come from error or impurity or by way of **deceit**; 4 but just as we have been **approved by God** to be entrusted with the gospel, so **we speak**, not as **pleasing** men, but **God who examines our hearts**. 5 For **we never came with flattering speech**, as you know, nor with a pretext for greed—God is witness— 6 nor did we seek glory from men, either from you or from others, even though as apostles of Christ we might have asserted our authority. 7 But **we proved to be gentle among** you, as a nursing mother tenderly cares for her own children. ... 11 just as you know how we were exhorting and encouraging and imploring each one of you **as a father would his own children**."*

Paul established in the short time he was in Thessalonica that he did not want to burden them with his expense, he was not a lazy man, and he did not work among them as some kind of ancient huckster or salesman. He worked hard, paid his way, and cared for them personally as he preached Biblically. The bottom line was this: He could call upon his TESTIMONY of life to back up his MESSAGE. Words are far more effective when they are rooted in a measured life that endeavors to live truth. If you are living in sexual sin, it is hard to correct a son or daughter who is about to make such a choice. They know you – and your life doesn't match your lofty words. If you cheat on your taxes, it won't be long until your voice cracks when you tell your teen not to cheat on their upcoming exam. Paul made clear that his life backed his message. He was not perfect, but he was no huckster, either. Words to the contrary may have been floating about – but Paul would have none of that left unanswered. We can be harmless in our response, but we need not flinch from clarifying attacks that are based on lies. If we represent truth, we must do so without apology – popular affirmation or not.

Fifth, Paul exhorted the believers:

From the beginning, the message was not only to come to Christ, but to be changed in their daily walk to a manner worthy of Jesus' payment for them (2:12; 3:12-13).

*He encouraged the believers to walk with God, not simply look at the Gospel as a "get out of Hell free" card. In 1 Thessalonians 2:12 he wrote: "...so **that you would walk in a manner worthy** of the God who calls you into His own kingdom and glory. He affirmed that as a core value in 3:12 when he wrote: "...and may the Lord cause **you to increase and abound in love for one another**, and **for all people**, just as we also do for you; 13 so that He may **establish your hearts without blame in holiness** before our God and Father at the coming of our Lord Jesus with all His saints."*

We made the point that Paul promised trouble rather than fill his presentation with personal benefit, but it is worth remembering that Paul also demanded surrender to Jesus in areas of behavior rather than emphasizing only the benefits of Heaven and security in our eternal state. Paul connected the message of the Gospel and the foundation of the church to a call to HOLY LIVING. Is that message what we hear proclaimed about us today? Paul's heart was exposed. He wanted believers to live like they were God's people – not self-indulgent princes and princesses that allowed their "felt needs" to direct their decisions. This will be even clearer in the second part of his letter, so we will reserve the discussion until then.

Sixth, Paul celebrated the news he received:

When Paul couldn't wait to hear from the new believers and know of their progress in Christ any longer, he sent Timothy - who eventually returned with a joyful report (3:1-3, 5-8).

In the opening three chapters of the book, Paul communicated excitement over the people that he received from the report

Timothy brought back to him. In 1 Thessalonians 3:1, Paul wrote:

"Therefore when we could endure it no longer, we thought it best to be left behind at Athens alone, 2 and we sent Timothy, ... 6 But now that Timothy has come to us from you, and has brought us good news of your faith and love, and that you always think kindly of us, longing to see us just as we also long to see you, 7 for this reason, brethren, in all our distress and affliction we were comforted about you through your faith; 8 for now we really live, if you stand firm in the Lord.

Who can mistake Paul's note of anxiousness concerning the people? He prayed and prayed, because like all of us, he was tempted to worry and worry. Paul was an Apostle, not a demi-god that wasn't afflicted with a sin nature and a desire to control what he could not. Don't make him such a good guy that you no longer see him as a regular Christian – struggling to trust God when things are falling apart. Remember what he had been suffering along the journey? Sometimes it seems God hides His control – when, in fact, what He is doing is working beyond our sight and in matters beyond our grasp. Paul heard back from Timothy, and celebration and joy flooded, tears flowed, and his prayer journal got some exclamation points scratched beside old requests!

The opening three chapters of the letter seem to offer a **description the permeation of the Gospel to the Thessalonians** during the three weeks of the mission team's tireless sharing and caring ministry, another **verified account of their forced exit** from the believers under duress and a record of **Timothy's dispatched trip** to check in. Apparently Paul agreed to have Timothy go while he was still alone in Athens during his darkest time of ministry. That left the Apostle without his team longer, but in the end it provided word from the fledgling church in Macedonia that so richly encouraged Paul. It's nice to end the section on a note of happy celebration, but Paul's letter had a second part as well.

The second part of the letter contained specific commands for the people to follow as they grew in the faith:

This section includes the **last two chapters of the letter** as the epistle is divided for us in our modern Bibles. Paul made clear that the commands were a continuation of his earlier "live" teaching, and that he expected the people to continue to grow in obedience and submission to the teachings as from God. In classic fashion, Paul made that clear at the very beginning of the section, found in 1 Thessalonians 4:1 when he wrote:

*"**Finally** then, brethren, **we request and exhort you** in the Lord Jesus, that **as you received from us instruction** as to **how** you ought **to walk** and please God (just as you actually do walk), that you **excel still more**. 2 For you know what **commandments** we gave you **by** the **authority of the Lord Jesus**."*

Paul wasn't unsure of what he taught, nor the source of the revealed truth – and he made that clear. A church that surrenders parts of their Bible in fear of looking un-scientific or a dread over charges of a text lacking historical integrity will also surrender moral precepts in the face of social pressure – it is inevitable. Paul asserted vigorously that his words were from God. If they weren't, he was lying. If he was telling a lie (or some editor inserted this idea later) than the Bible is not a good book, but a book of lies. It won't lead you to Heaven – if such a place exists. It cannot tell you about your Creator – if there is one. My point is that the surrender of the text is a BIG DEAL to our faith – because our faith is rooted completely within it. The earlier church used phrases like: "The Bible is our only rule for faith and practice." In modern churches where that idea has been surrendered, it is but a matter of time when they lose all coherence and consistency in their practice, and become a lump of clay molded not by a Heavenly potter, but by earthly pressures to allow the mold its influence.

What were these essential commands to which the Apostle pointed them? Let me suggest the **three that seem to "stick out"** more than others:

First, there was the command to live a life of sexual purity (4:3-8).

1 Thessalonians 4:3 states: "For this is the will of God, your sanctification; that is, that you abstain from sexual immorality; 4 that each of you know how to possess his own vessel in sanctification and honor, 5 not in lustful passion, like the Gentiles who do not know God; 6 and that no man transgress and defraud his brother in the matter because the Lord is the avenger in all these things, just as we also told you before and solemnly warned you. 7 For God has not called us for the purpose of impurity, but in sanctification. 8 So, he who rejects this is not rejecting man but the God who gives His Holy Spirit to you."

Paul flatly stated sexual purity as a core value of the early church, and a revealed truth from God above. He called us to "sanctification" a word that means "to be set apart." Lest that not be clear, he followed with another restatement in verses four and five, that a believer is NOT to be like the world around them in this area. As he developed the thought, he told them in verse six that relationships between them were to be held as a high value, and that sensual behaviors would "defraud" others in the family of God. He made clear that God intended distinction in this area, and that rejecting the cause of purity was not an option as a believer.

Here again I find myself wondering if Paul would recognize the modern church as "Christian" in its value system.

Purity is encouraged when we carefully delineate how attraction is not the same as action.

God placed desires within us – we were created with some intrinsic desires. At the same time, we live in a fallen state. As a result, we must be very careful not to see those desires as something "naturally good." Man is broken inside, and his desires reflect that brokenness. We must continually make clear a Biblical truth – wanting something is not the same as acting on a desire. The Bible begins with simple restriction of action – but eventually calls the maturing believer to surrender the very desires themselves. When we "grow up" in our faith, we won't excuse our sin by claiming desire had the determining place in our decision making process. **We will see God's will, not our want, as the most important factor**.

Purity is encouraged when we help young women understand the value of developing their inner spirit as well as keeping a healthy body.

With a fashion world designed to pry money from your wallet and promising to make you look "hot" – it has become even more important for the church to carefully help young women to see that the body will not retain its God-given youthful beauty forever. We get older or we die on the path. The fact is, we are on the planet for a short time compared to eternity. If the Christian message is true, our submission to Jesus is based on two things: first we acknowledge that Jesus is our Lord and we offer Him our whole self. Second, we submit because we know that our Savior knows what is best. He knows what we do not about the plan, the future and our best life in His presence in eternity. In the end purity is encouraged when we teach men and women to see eternal things as more important than temporal ones.

Purity is encouraged when we place safeguards on our young men at home and restrict their unlimited access to websites and media that encourage immoral sexual pursuits.

Because we have redefined the word "adult" in the context of sexuality as "removal of restraint" in our society, the church must clearly mark out that ADULT truly means "under control". It is a CHILD that throws a tantrum when unhappy. An adult should know better. We must apply that same logic to other urges. Children punch and punch back. Adults shouldhave better control of their hands. We must make the case that guardrails and restrictions aren't to stop young people from growing – they are to provide sufficient time for that young person to grow the necessary disciplines before thrown to predators that lurk across the wireless signals.

A second command was offered - to work hard and stay out of other people's business (4:9-12).

1 Thessalonians 4:9 Now as to the love of the brethren, you have no need for anyone to write to you... 10 ...But we urge you, brethren, to excel still more, 11 and to make it your ambition to lead a quiet life and attend to your own business and work with your hands, just as we commanded you, 12 so that you will behave properly toward outsiders and not be in any need.

It may astound modern Christians to know that **Paul intended believers to get a job, work in that job and avoid making other people pay their way**. In fact, the Apostle made the point that a believer's ability to take care of others and live quietly at work was very much a part of their Christian faith. We need not meddle from the pulpit; we have Scripture before us that challenges any who would see a way around work as God's plan. There are disabilities that need to be taken into account – but I suggest this is an extreme much less frequent than claimed – even by believers. We cannot enshrine laziness in some kind of reward system and expect anything less than an increasing number of unproductive people. When there is a true need, a believer is not wrong to access the provision for that need – but we must be very wary here of expecting others to pay our way through life. Some people are simply unsure of a truth: Life is hard. Work is not always fun. Since the expulsion from the garden every job was given its weeds. We must be careful to check any thinking that would argue that everyone has is easier than we do. **In many, if not most cases, some of our difficulty was added by our own earlier life choices**.

A third command was issued - to comfort one another with the truth concerning death and life (4:13-5:11).

It seems from reading 1 Thessalonians 4:13-15 that some believers felt those who died in Christ were somehow penalized – a notion the Apostle quickly dismissed in the letter. Paul wanted to make sure the "uninformed" were made to understand that those believers who died actually have a better place in line of the resurrection of the dead. The timing of that resurrection are as follows:

1 Thessalonians 4:16 "For the Lord Himself will descend from heaven with a [m]shout, with the voice of the archangel and with the trumpet of God, and the dead in Christ will rise first. 17 Then we who are alive and remain will be caught up together with them in the clouds to meet the Lord in the air, and so we shall always be with the Lord. 18 Therefore comfort one another with these words.

Paul wanted to make it clear that when Jesus returned to the earth to take His own, He would do so in the order of those who died BEFORE those who are alive. To the believer, death is no penalty, but a mere illustration that the fallen world has not yet been fully redeemed. When Christ makes all things new, death will be forever banished to the hole of the fiery pit. The rest of the section in 1 Thessalonians 5:1-11 reminded the believers that the world would not believe that Jesus would return, but would focus all their attention on THIS world. Believers should be awake and alert in their times, and actively comforting one another with the truth that (as Martin Luther wrote): "the body they may kill, God's truth abideth still – His kingdom is forever!"

Missions Instructor Gregory Fisher of Victory Bible College wrote of his earlier times in West Africa: "What will he say when he shouts?" The question took me by surprise. I had already found that West African Bible College students can ask some of the most penetrating questions about minute details of Scripture. "Reverend, I Thess. 4:16 says that Christ will descend from heaven with a loud command. I would like to know what that command will be." I wanted to leave the question unanswered, to tell him that we must not go past what Scripture has revealed, but my mind wandered to an encounter I had earlier in the day with a refugee from the Liberian civil war. The man, a high school principal, told me how he was apprehended by a two-man death squad. After several hours of terror, as the men described how they would torture and kill him, he narrowly escaped. After hiding in the bush for two days, he was able to find his family and escape to a neighboring country. The escape cost him dearly: two of his children lost their lives. The stark cruelty unleashed on an unsuspecting, undeserving population had touched me deeply. I also saw flashbacks of the beggars that I pass each morning on my way to the office. Every day I see how poverty destroys dignity, robs men of the best of what it means to be human, and sometimes substitutes the worst of what it means to be an animal. I am haunted by the vacant eyes of people who have lost all hope. "Reverend, you have not given me an answer. What will he say?" The question hadn't gone away. "Enough!'" I said. "He will shout, 'Enough' when he returns." A look of surprise opened the face of the student. "What do you mean, 'Enough'?" "Enough suffering. Enough starvation. Enough terror. Enough death. Enough indignity. Enough lives trapped in hopelessness. Enough sickness and disease. Enough time. Enough".

I don't know if the missionary is correct about that, but I wouldn't be surprised! Life here is broken, but God is working a plan – and Paul showed that plan to be at work in him as he shared a short "Postcard from the edge" with the Thessalonians. He was hurt, but he was healing. He was beaten up, but he was not quitting. **A mature believer lives his values and follows under pressure, recognizing God is at work even when times are tough.**

Other volumes in the series through the Bible are available through amazon.com and can be found by searching for:

"Dr. Randall D. Smith"

Free teaching resources are also available at:

www.randalldsmith.com